TO FETCH A
PAIL OF WATER

JILL STANLEY

WESTBOW
PRESS®
A DIVISION OF THOMAS NELSON
& ZONDERVAN

WestBow Press books may be ordered through booksellers or by contacting:

WestBow Press
A Division of Thomas Nelson & Zondervan
1663 Liberty Drive
Bloomington, IN 47403
www.westbowpress.com
1 (866) 928-1240

ISBN: 978-1-5127-1576-7 (sc)
ISBN: 978-1-5127-1577-4 (e)

Library of Congress Control Number: 2015916685

Print information available on the last page.

WestBow Press rev. date: 10/20/2015

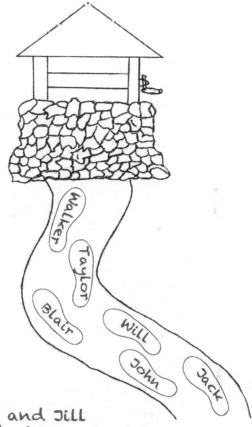

Jack and Jill
climbed many hills
to fetch a pail of water.

Jill broke her crown
in many a town,
But the Hound of heaven
always found her.

My lovely ones...

Thank you for providing your unique serendipities and enriching my life beyond measure. We have dipped our lives in plenteous polka-dot places, many of those *not* ones we would have ever chosen, but the well has never run dry of pregnant opportunities! Through tears and laughter, wailing and rejoicing, we are still one family, glued together with the mortar of shared experiences: tough but tender times, losing but winning, for each of us carries a bucket-full of love and loyalty. May the roads that separate our lives be only glory-bound ribbons that bind our hearts as one.

Jack...my JEWEL, my elephant... a tower I have run to, for he shows me Jesus

John... my JOY, my first-born ...entered our world with a be-doze and a hammer in his hand; quick-witted

Will...my WARRIOR...quiet strength...Jesus must need your testimony, for you are a rock

Blair...my BEAUTY-FULL one...from pig-tails and smocked dresses to prudence, yet such a spicy delight

Taylor...my TENDERHEARTED one...gentle, yet tough; tenacious and determined; thrifty but carefree

Walker...my WREATH...you decorate my days in unexpected ways, laying a welcome mat for *anything*

Kyle, Katie, Nan...sisters by birth, yet soul-mates in spirit; Jennifer, Missy, Reggie, Ally...big hugs

Alyssa, Melaine, Mills, Molli, Sam, Sarah, Cole, Jillian, Nolan, unborn ones...stay underneath His feathers

Harriet Mills, Joan Hartman, Debbie Moore, Becky Bourne, Carol Girsky, Becky Torbett, Emily Spencer...For sisterly encouragement and sweet fellowship, a grace gift that overwhelms me

Jesus...my Gentle Giant...You never ever have given up on me. How grateful I am. Thank You for wooing me through all my temper tantrums, pity parties and DIY projects. I love You.

CONTENTS

PREFACE

Put clothes in the dryer. Start another load. Let the dogs out. Again. Patch hole in back fence where the beagle dug her way to freedom. Again. Beatrice, can't live with you, can't live without you. Take meat out of freezer for supper. Load dishwasher. Exercise. The bedroom chair, perched with clean, albeit wrinkled clothes, begs release from its load. Oh, isn't that how my heart feels?

Why the procrastination? That's not me. I am the early-o'clock-scholar, the one whose project is all tethered together before the sun finds its resting place, the one who always follows every period in the directions, the champion of organizing chaos!

Not today, please. Company's comin' in three days, the Bible study group yearns for a tasty dessert, Jean's curtains call out to be stitched. "Jill".....the whisper is repeated. Again. Words from the shelter of my mama's wings, as she read *If Jesus Came to my House*,[1] hammer a familiar message, and my soul is nailed with conviction. Jesus is occupying my cozy rocking chair, patiently watching me dance around many duties. "But, Lord, who *really* cares? *Everyone* is texting; blogging; tweeting; linking in; pondering, perusing, and posting facebook entries; instagramming each inebriating incident. Opining on the minors, thinking it's the majors. Why, 794 "friends" don't need one more parcel of data to overload frenzied lives."

Just put one thought in front of another. He began this story long before I played "house" under the willow tree, watching Mama hang loads of laundry on the clothesline. "In returning and rest you shall be saved" (from the pitfalls of procrastination). "In quietness and confidence shall be your strength" (I choose to dwell in Your shadow). Isaiah 30:15, NKJ, parenthesis mine.

Hush, my soul, and savor the sweetness. "Though the Lord gives you the bread of adversity and the water of affliction, (enigmas need not remain riddles), He *will* still be with you to teach you. (Hallelujah, my burden is in the basket!) ...your Teacher will not be moved into a corner anymore, (marveling at His moves in retrospect), and your ears *shall* hear a word behind you, saying, 'This is the way, walk in it'." (I wave the white flag. His banner over me is love.) Isaiah 30:20-21, NKJ, parenthesis and italics mine. I *choose* the pen, for my story has already been written in red; I simply must testify and herald His enterprise in investing in me. And I cannot stop. If I say that I'll put a bushel over the Lord's light, "His Word was in my heart like a burning fire shut up in my bones. I am weary of holding it back. And I cannot." Jeremiah 20:9, NKJ.

"Now, go, write it on a tablet before them. Inscribe it on a scroll, that it may serve in a time to come as a *witness* forever." Isaiah 30:8, NASB.

1

This is the House That Jack Built

Four-tenths of one mile. That's all. The distance that separates my house from this gem. She sits perched all alone on the county road, but she has won my heart, for I have danced in her shoes. She is mired down in red Georgia clay, muddied with the filth of life, covered with a cloak to prevent rainy days from poking any more holes in her soul, and terribly lonely from a lack of laughter. Tattered and torn with age, her beauty is deep beyond the countenance she exhibits. Spread on her perch of eminence, yet mostly unknown to the bustling brood of daily travelers. But isn't that just like Jesus?

In our love affair we trade intimate touching moments from past birthday celebrations. I understand her tragedy but revel in her triumphs. I can hear her children's laughter as games are fashioned in the front yard. Dirt Ball Canyon in my youth is paralleled by her tractor and tobacco-hanging tales. A bond has been established that has oozed into the very marrow of the meshed fabric of our experiences, each thread carefully pulled from decades of our separateness.

The stories she has shared are all in my suppositions, but our commonalities keep us both candid about our past, each remembrance adding a piece of the scaffolding supporting the spine of our purposes. After all, everyone has a story. Even though adventures are varied, like colored polka-dots on girly tee-shirts, each detail has been sifted through the magnanimous hands of a compassionate Father, as He woos lovingly in each ear.

I have many notes written and pasted in corners of books, my Bible, the dining room silver drawer, the guest bedroom dresser, and mostly in my mind; saving the thought of encouragement and neglecting the giver's epithet, I covet being able to resurrect names of many who have added to my spiritual journey. One such Unknown Soldier in my armory of scribbled memos articulated how dear ones are tied with love. "When one communicates with another, something meaningful happens to you. A bond has been established that is instantaneous; degrees of separateness are cut down to zero. Stories are the ramparts we build against isolationism and loneliness." Friends can grow separately without growing apart. So...even though I recently met you, I have known you long, dear new friend. And all friends have names: you have been dubbed Qaneh...the broken reed.[2] As we have commiserated these last few years, this Tennessee girl now has Georgia clay under her fingernails!

I ask the Lord to bless my paths, the steps I take, the doors I enter. But stones have often tripped me, weeds have choked out my movements, doors have been marked "Keep Out".

I have always been a DIY girl – pick up the pieces, clean up the mess, play the cards you're dealt, rig it up another way, get it all together. When the going gets tough, the tough just gets going. And don't forget the smiley face!

Well, these walls are not so firm; they haven't always kept trouble out. The roof has leaked. The door has not always swung open to welcome joy. Its windows have blocked heavenly light. The hearth has been known to funnel smoke *in*, not *up*. Pure and free from sin I am not, but He has been faithful to keep on keepin' on until this construction project conforms to His pleasure.

Fruit ripens slowly; days of sunshine and storms both do their share to complete the maturing. Mamas and daddies love on their babies, then babies fall down and get boo-boos. Children learn to ride bikes without training wheels, but freedom is cut short when the speed limit is broken.

My mama and daddy saw that we four girls were religiously in Sunday School. Daddy owned a small drug store on the town square. Grace was said before meals, dollars were dropped in the collection plate, but Jesus-talk was rare. We walked or rode our bikes the four blocks to grammar school, parking our transportation in the bike racks in front of school. Never did it occur to any of us that our vehicle wouldn't be there seven hours later; and they were! Skipping through the front doors, we were greeted by creaky old wooden floors, cloak rooms, and large winding staircases. Recess was held romping in the "jungle", whirling on the merry-go-round, jumping rope to school-girl chants, or swinging up to the sky. Mrs. Reynolds' lunchroom provided yummy chocolate cake. Junior high sent basketball's Mr. Shoaf and PE shows and Mr. Akers' "talks" on growing up, to which we girls would snicker and roll our eyes.

But, why do I often remember the embarrassments and disappointments over the idealistic life we led? I prayed so hard for two uncles, both in their thirties, who died anyway, leaving my cousins all alone. Mama entered this pig-tailed gal in some beauty pageant at the Ruffin Theatre, but I was not beautiful enough to be called to walk the runway again. Miss Ermine requested that I play in her piano recital, but I botched "Jesu, Joy of Man's Desiring" so badly that I left the church in tears. She could make me play once, but she couldn't make me fail twice! Cheerleader try-outs ended in failure. I remember clearly the look on Daddy's face after I pulled on the curtain rod cord, before he finished installing the den drapes. Explaining why I was kicked out of the Friday night movie for a few giggles among friends took me nowhere; I was grounded anyway.

Joining in with Presbyterian protocol, I made a profession of faith in Jesus Christ on Easter Sunday with the rest of my seventh grade class. However, while exiting a Pioneer junior high Bible study several months later, I vividly recall an incident half-way down the steps behind the church "sanctuary". In a whispered echo just to me, I heard or perceived, "What's the big deal? You are a good person! Why do you think you need all this church stuff?" For the longest period of time, y-e-a-r-s, I held my act together. The foundation appeared strong and solid; cracks can remain undetected for quite some time to all but the most Discerning Eye.

If my soul had truly loosed itself, I would have a different tale to tell, for "I do not do the good I want to do, but I practice the evil that I do not want to do." Romans 7:19, HCSB. Never could I gain the victory my heart desired. On the outside painted shutters, shiny windows, blossoming flowers. On the inside closets stuffed full of unworn clothes, junk crammed under the bed, out-dated food in the pantry.

Spring flowers faded; fall colors ushered in high school days. Mr. Hughes algebra class and my first bad report card grade. Junior English persuasion writing assignment; my choosing to speak on Jesus, only to be told I was not mature enough to be judging such matters. Miss Thurmond's crazy Latin conjugations. Mr. Science Guy allowing the science class to blow up the lab. And the steady attention of a junior boy!

After dating through high school, my finishing college, and his having a year of dental school under his belt, we married. Teaching third grade and being a wife were going to make me complete! Church was on our agenda but not Jesus. Trouble lurked like a prowling lion in my soul. My tummy would knot up, mostly at night, and, often in a stage of extreme restlessness, my body would quiver. What was there to dread? I had what I wanted!

One midnight, enough became enough; I crept into the apartment living room, knelt on the floor, and begged Jesus to save me from this bondage. The very next morning, on my way to school, the old voice I'd encountered a decade ago on the church steps, whispered again, "Why just look at you! You're *no* different than you were yesterday! You're the same today that you were yesterday! The very idea that you thought that that god of yours could help you!" Even having gone to Sunday School for 18 years had not taught me exactly what I was being saved *from*. Indeed, *there was nothing* I could tell that was different. I had no new excitement this Friday morning, no new power, no new knowledge. Zapped by the wizard's wand, I surmised that I would be transformed...right then! Spit out wisdom like a vending machine. Jolly like Santa Claus. Maybe the voice was right. So....when the light turned green at the corner of Yale and Raleigh-Millington Road, the life that had Jesus had re-created the night before in an upstairs room at 3825 Jackson Avenue, drove into an insidiously slow quicksand of fallacy and defeat.

My druggist daddy brought my second "savior". Even though married life was pleasurable, it didn't fabricate happiness, so maybe a bottle of pills would, at the very least, allow life to resume some kind of normalness, whatever that truly meant. The pill bottle became more valuable than car keys; I played "What if...?" The meds were not overused, but they *were* security. "Why can't I *feel* You? Why don't You just show up somehow and tell me what to *do*?" Like my friend down the road, my shiny window panes began to reveal the world's dirt, and one pane even blew out, as if a baseball had given a child an "uh-oh" moment.

But new circumstances were on the horizon! The dentist graduated. We moved to a small town 15 miles from home and family. Two precious boys. A newly constructed dream house. Country club membership. An invitation to join the bridge club. I had arrived! For awhile, several years, Eden distracted my attention. This 3300 square foot house was so much fun to decorate. Flooring, stained glass, fabric, paint colors, goodies to recreate into fascinating treasures from junk and antique places I haunted. A breath of heaven!

If I had only been so diligent in coloring my spirit! The idol of worldly nature hid the torture of a fleshly soul. His promises are so true and sure, but feelings overrule a naive soul. The dentist worked two nights a week at the state prison near-by, and it was during those hours of twilight that my frail emotions were entertained by an invisible fear. Lying on my knees, I feared someone would come and carry me off to Bolivar (a psychiatric hospital). Panic attacks hit often, momentarily sucking out life. "Sit by the door at church, just in case"; "grab a few items at the grocery store and check out while the line is empty "; "If I can make it to the (Hatchie River) bridge (half-way home), I'll be OK."

Little did I know that the Lord was wooing me, the perfect gentleman who will not force Himself into a heart. Rocking away as I cooked, keeping nightmares out of my closet, laundering my filthy garments, I began begging Him for relief from this burden on my back. I did not thank Him, nor delight in His constant protection. I dwelt outside His shelter, walked distantly from His shadow; He chased me, seeking to shield me with His feathers, but I would not accept refuge under the wings. Reference to Psalm 91:1,4, NASB. Needing someone to guide me on the heavenly path, my answer to church people would have been sarcastic. "Well, how can I understand unless someone guides me?" Acts 8:31, NASB.

It would be 15 years later, yes, y - e – a – r - s, when I heard Ron Dunn preach in Fort Worth, Texas, that God graciously granted me the "A-HA" moment that my lonely heart was craving. In a sermon entitled "God's Surprises", he plainly unraveled tangled threads of misunderstandings. The story of Jacob's night-long wrestling match with the angel of God (pre-incarnate Jesus) still will tutor humble learners. It has been, indeed will continue to be, a struggle of growth and maturity until the break of day. Because of a lack of care for my friend Qaneh down the road, the door is bolted and cautions: "Do Not Enter". Rusty old tin roofing bars entrance to abandoned barns.

But our Abba Father is faithful to keep on keepin' on with us. He never bolts the doors to keep us away, even though He allows us to slam the door on His invitations. Although we surmise that the devil is a hard task-master, God Himself hands us our toughest undertakings. I can announce a hearty "No" to the old fibber much easier than I can confess a sincere gracious "Yes, Lord," to Jesus.

Often interruptions of our expectations of "how life should be" are hurled forcefully downward, even though Abba had pre-planned for that surprise to bless, not curse, us. The perceived curse becomes a "monster to be moved and/or disposed of; how arduous the task to allow the monster to be a minister!"[3] Dr. David Jeremiah's definition of faith has sustained me in many seasons: believing in advance what only makes sense in reverse.[4] Jacob held onto the angel all through the rough night and didn't let go until he was enriched by the experience. At 97 years of age, the determination Jacob exhibited blesses me.

But... as I currently wallowed in the floor, my cries begged Him to take away this agony, so that I could go on with life's routines. MY routine!!! My blessing would be the gift, not the Giver. The present, not the Presenter. Only in retrospect can I gaze agape at the written Word, words I wouldn't treasure until I searched for them.

Jacob named the battle site "Penuel", which means "Face of God".[5] Genesis 32:30. However, he still faced a rocky road. On his way home with his family caravan to reunite with his brother Esau after an estranged 21 years, Jacob's emotions fought a battle with God's promises. Before he had left Penuel, God rehearsed with him His command and covenant promise to bless his family for generations to come. God even gave Jacob a new name: "'Israel': for you have striven with God and men and have prevailed." Genesis 32:28, NASB. Oh, that I would wait for Him with such unction and perseverance! The lumber in Qaneh would not succumb to rot, the roof would not spring a leak, and the hearth would blaze anew with a hot vigor.

Another assignment He was echoing in those days was one of confidently expecting Him to act. "Do you truly believe what you confess or do you doubt like the ocean waves? Will you walk with Me in daily surrender and dependence?" This lesson is one that cannot, c-a-n-n-o-t be overlooked. It is crucial to learn before the foundation can support weight. Good and bad run on parallel tracks and usually arrive at the same time!! Will I take all of life as it arrives day by day and never hit the pause button? Like Jacob, what I name a place is what I will get out of it. Although weathered and worn, Qaneh still holds her head high.

2

Little Bo Peep Has Lost Her Sheep

Parallel tracks of His wooing. Good and bad. "Consider it ALL joy, my friends, when you encounter various trials, knowing (nailed down) that the testing of your faith produces endurance. Let endurance have its perfect result, that you may be perfect and complete (grow up)." James 1:2-4, NASB, parenthesis mine. Better or worse. Pleasure or pain. Valleys or mountain-tops. Questions or certainties.

April 23. Only a week ago the news arrived that I was pregnant with our third child. Traveling the fifteen miles to deliver good news, little did I suspect that in a brief few days my mama would travel those same miles in reverse to impart tragic tidings. Daddy had completed suicide after a lengthy battle with depression. Only 59 years young, troubling times had hit the drug store; several sundry circumstances had blotched his ability to provide.

On April 22 he had agreed to be admitted to the hospital, so, as I tucked my seven year old John into bed, he voiced this prayer: "Please, God, help my Jack 'pass his tests' because I love him so much." The tests never got administered, for he shot himself at the end of the bed he'd shared with my mama for 35 years. "Thank You, Lord, his agony is over." I hope so, oh, I hope so, for I *need* him to welcome me home one day soon.

He was a gentle giant. My memories of his kissing all five of us girls every time he came home; of his crazy photographs, especially the one with the Christmas bow on his head; of his loud colored socks; of his golf dates with Bert and Jack Carter and his always stopping by the pool to watch us swim; of his big smelly cigar and can of sardines, top rolled back by its key; of his handy-man skills and his garage haven; all these memories give me comfort that he truly loved us dearly, albeit he never learned how to healthily handle conflict. The number of years that I have loved him from afar is greater than those in which I had him near. Why, the life I carried inside of me that day is a mother herself...twice! Years *do* ease pain, but every April 23, every April 27 (his birthday), every Father's Day, every grandchild milestone brings sweet melancholy.

Parallel tracks. Good and bad. November 12. Elizabeth ("God is an oath"-the absolute faithful One) Blair entered our world. But the bounteous blessing of these three children traveled alongside a crumbling foundation. Qaneh began to visibly crumble after seasons of a hungry termite invasion. Two months before my blonde beauty turned two, on the eve of a seventh birthday celebration for our son Will, I heard the verdict: d-i-v-o-r-c-e. An olio of unbelief, panic, and wild imaginings set my teeth on edge. "What will happen to us? God, where are You? I will wake up, and realize that it was just a bad dream." The pain of Daddy's death still rearing its ugly head, I began to deeply grieve that these three young children would not grow up with the stability of care-free and fun childhood times. I cannot relay each child's story because God has no grandchildren, but for 30 years the memory of a birthday celebration turned tragic has indelibly etched scars across my mind's eye.

But, here again, God was lovingly pulling me to His side, begging for me to allow Him to be my Abba. I wanted no part of this wilderness.

Again, though, in times yet to come, Ron Dunn would be used to open my eyes. In Genesis Abraham went through several crises in his faith journey. "It was a matter of God bringing Abraham where He wanted him to be. Walking with God *always* involves leaping/losing one thing to take hold of another."[6] How hard the lesson was for me to acutely learn, to appropriate my environment with His call. Still I wasn't a good student. I'd have to re-enroll in His class. Where was a mentor to encourage, to reprimand my untamed choices? When my five children, their spouses, and 9+ grandchildren read these ink markings called letters, will their hearts witness my teardrops? The school of hard knocks is a tough road, but there is also great treasure to be found in the wisdom of having trod a well-worn path. "Eye has not seen, nor ear heard, nor have entered into the heart of man the things which God has prepared for those who love Him." I Corinthians 2:9, NKJ.

The path I chose was totally out of character for a Jesus-follower. The hurt clamped down on my attitude, and I became bitter, not better; for six long years I was a refrigerator, sated with junk food; a tsunami-torn island that spew the volcanic rock of my misfortune on any poor soul who ventured near. But He was still wooing, still mowing grass, still feeding the dog, still repainting chipped woodwork, still providing manna and living water. I just didn't have the appetite.

Parallel tracks. Hang on or let go. We only grow up when we give up. We go without knowing, just as Abraham left his home for the Promised Land. Was it a day's journey or months? Years? How will we eat? What will happen if....? We won't have answers until we see God's hand in retrospect, either in the rear-view mirror or in heaven. Corrie ten Boom said, "Hold everything loosely, for it hurts too deeply when He pries your fingers loose" and again, "No pit is so deep that He is not deeper still." His promise of a new home was much more voluptuous for Abraham than dwelling in the world's tents.

Qaneh, although rust and moth have eaten away at your outward beauty, you are still called home by the little boy/ grown man who played ball in your yard and now lives across the road.

Parallel tracks. Hold close or give up. My dream house was sold to another family; no longer would I battle the back yard kudzu which threatened to devour me. So much time and energy spent clutching a prized idol.

Parallel tracks. Absurdity or prudence. How do I form letters and words to convey the reasoning of the single most asinine ridiculous decision I ever knew anyone to make? Like the choice animals Abraham brought to God in Genesis 15, my children were my AAA choice. Physically Abraham slew his unblemished, his choice first-born animals, but I killed their spirit. As the dentist and I sat in our hollowed out living room dividing hay, wood, and stubble, he relayed to me that he *needed* the boys to live with him. "I feel so fragile emotionally that I don't know how I will handle this." The Goliath word s-u-i-c-i-d-e was not physically mentioned, but I *knew* what had been intimated. Oh, God, please do not summon me to the "S" trial again?? Irrational, yes, insane emotions birthed themselves as I mulled this dilemma. If ever one had a nightmare where an Indian was chasing the cowboy, knowing that, if caught, his head would be another tee-pee trophy, this was it.

But, John and Will would be only a couple of blocks away. I would get them from school every day. I can still help coach the soccer team. And I will not be declared guilty of abetting this hara-kiri.

As I sit writing this, the Holy Spirit has given me an assurance of something I had not considered. Abraham believed the Lord's promise that he would live in the Promised Land, so God gave him an extraordinary picture of His covenant love. The animals were laid out in two sections, Abraham fell asleep, and "terror and great darkness fell on him. God said, 'Know for certain that your descendants will be strangers in a land that is not theirs, where they will be enslaved and oppressed for 400 years'...Then there appeared a flaming torch which passed between the pieces. On that day the Lord made a covenant with Abram saying, 'To your descendants I *have (already) given* this land, from the river of Egypt as far as the great River Euphrates'." Genesis 15:12-18, NASB, parenthesis mine.

Ron Dunn once said that holy fear comes before holy joy. God wounds then heals. He humbles then lifts up. Egypt is a picture of darkness, but He sets us free. God did not ask Abram to give anything. He never lifted a finger after he fetched what God asked for. He gave up a few animals to gain heaven. My boys indeed were laid bare by their mother, but, He is in the pottery business. Clay is available, unformed, and moldable. He works from the inside out. He forms the way He pleases, makes sure the impurities are removed, and keeps His foot on the turning wheel until the vessel is just right. He is much more interested in character than in our contentment, so pressure is good. We laid them in the jaws of a vise, but God can...indeed, He WILL... redeem my foolish naivety with a fantastic newness of life.

Parallel tracks. Survive or thrive. In a tiny basement apartment, I found God through a friend who propped up my sagging foundation with her sweet Jesus-spirit. The ogre of her adversity had already been chopped up with her machete, and the jungle of parasitic vines had wilted and withered, so she handled me as a mother with a feverish child. "Blessed be the God and Father of our Lord Jesus Christ, the Father of mercies and God of **all** comfort. He comforts us in **all** our afflictions, so that we may be able to comfort those who are in **any** kind of affliction, through the comfort we ourselves receive from God." 2 Corinthians 1:3-5, HCSB, bold print mine.

We walked together, cooked together, laughed and cried together. And she loved my children. Funny thing, she and another close friend had both been victorious in a battle I was still waging. What was mature in one of them I soaked in, and then the other gave generously in another aspect, so together they glued me back together.

In less time than the school year is long, all three children were together again under my roof. The dentist relayed that his week-end warrior duty was probably going to be full-time; if so, he would be moving. Their belongings were packed up pronto.

Parallel tracks. Construct or raze. Erect or demolish. My oldest John was born with dirt under his fingernails. The words "be-doze" (bulldozer) and "goose-neck" were lilted from the cradle. His fascination with building and construction equipment dominated his youngest days. As he grew almost as tall as I am, he could have been found after school hanging around the lumber yard. The owner noticed his enthrallment and graciously offered him a paycheck for a bit of labor. Because of this association, notice reached my ears that the owner was developing a new subdivision near the school in which I was teaching. Early in the planning stages, I found the blueprints for a small salt-box and was granted the opportunity to choose the fixtures and colors. The mustiness of the basement apartment molted into a fresh pristine newness; an aura of confidence slithered into the broken crevices of my soul. The open wound scars over. Heralding spring, the crocus raises its head every March. Without fail, rays of morning sun dance across the bedroom window. "I will restore to you the years that the swarming locusts have eaten!" Joel 2:25, NKJV.

Parallel lines. Drink from bitter waters of Marah or be sated with the Living Spring. Relinquish Ishmael to gain Isaac.

Possessing "my" new house did not mean that I owned it, for on the horizon rose another drought. Qaneh, the reed, bent a bit the day the bank called...no she forfeited chunks of foundation. She was hurled through the night to the Land of Oz. After hitting solid rock again, I, like Dorothy, ventured outside to see in the daylight what the night had delivered. My banker had called to inform me that the dentist had declared bankruptcy, so the bank would need my not-paid-for car! "Lord, how in the world do You expect me to get to work? You know that there is more month than money!" My transportation lifeline had been unplugged.

Naomi ("pleasant"), her husband Elimelech, and their two sons had fled their Bethlehem ("House of Bread") home when famine hit. Traveling into enemy territory (a wise choice?), they expected to live there only temporarily. However, each son married a foreign woman (taboo!), both of whom were worshipers of Chemosh (children sacrificers) and perennial foes of the Jews. All three men died in Moab, and Naomi decided to go "home". Her daughter-in-law Ruth ("friendship") had become a follower of Jehovah God, so Ruth begged Naomi to be allowed to be her companion. "Where you go, I will go, and where you lodge, I will lodge. Your people will be my people and your God my God." Ruth 1:16, NASB.

Parallel lines. Pleasant or bitter. Flowers or weeds. Roses or thorns. As the two entered Bethlehem, Naomi's friends and family greeted them warmly, but Naomi retorted, "Do not call me Naomi, but Mara, for the Almighty has dealt bitterly with me. I went out full, but the Lord has brought me back empty." Ruth 1:20, NASB. Empty. Excuse me! Who is that you have alongside? Ruth just surrendered her entire birth family, culture, and god for you, and you treat her like a no-body? Again, I learned from Ron Dunn: "often our journey choices are determined by what we name each place."

My reaction to another loss was exactly like Naomi's. A fire-spewing volcano unleashed all its pent-up lava; my lovely little cottage overheard me rant and rave, and she witnessed me raise a fist to God's unwanted gift. How could something so bad have any good? Are you playing hide-and-seek? Jehovah was getting my full attention, albeit in a negative manner. Anger, yes, but at least the ashes of my heart would soon become a thing of beauty. To all who wait on the Lord, He will give "a crown of beauty instead of ashes, festive oil instead of mourning, and splendid clothes instead of despair. And they will be called righteous trees, planted by the Lord, to glorify Him." Isaiah 61:3, HCSB.

For the first time I can truthfully say that I was totally honest with Him. "Why have You taken away from me all the guys I have ever loved? I try and try to 'do' everything right, just to get knocked down again!" All the while He let me vent, never issuing a shred of condemnation, and then pulled me under the protection of His wings.

What if Elimilech had joined his loved ones in earnest prayer before he uprooted them to Moab? Of all places, why go to the people descended from Lot's incestuous relationship with his daughters? Unshackled or chained. Beauty from ashes. God wanted us to know that all nations are welcome to call on His name, and that He sometimes singles out seemingly unimportant people at insignificant times to use for His perfect purposes. It happens, even in spite of our poor choices, that He vividly displays Himself. Ruth, a no-body, a Moabitess, an enemy of the Hebrews, would be His choice to be the great grandmother of King David, and ultimately a woman whose children would bear Jesus Christ.

I did purchase a small used car but without knowing how the budget (mostly just how could the check stretch that far) would fare. Season follows season. School recessed for the summer, so, I began to seek employment to work off the loan. One of the manufacturing/distribution plants in town was adding workers to pick orders for car parts and accessories. Slinging tailpipes into necessary bins and packing crates for delivery to retailers in 100 degree temperatures was really very liberating, for frustrations soared upward through ceiling fans into oblivion. It became quite beautiful to die. Exhaustion always leads to a good night's sleep. My son Will had a good friend, whose mother stepped in to open her home to the children. What a Jesus we have in a friend! The car was half paid for at August's end, so maybe one more summer...

Fall to winter to spring....our houses change to celebrate birthdays and seasons, all the while the "bones" of the abode wait in silence, smiling as we laugh and comforting us as we cry. Working one night on a detailed cross-stitch, counting little crosses, changing thread colors, deleting scattered boxes, I felt frustrated and unproductive. How can something that will appear so lovely outwit me so? Rip it out, recount...it suddenly seemed so simple...if I would work from the inside out instead of out to in, it would simplify the process and plait the braided strands smoothly. Isn't that just how God works in our lives?

Don't insist on my own way. He is so much more intent on my being like Him in my core than on my striving to work myself to Him. Let go and let God.

The following summer found me back with my buggy, dancing up and down concrete aisles, hoping for a quick breeze to give me respite in the draining heat. But the heat on the August note-burning party was a welcome celebration! One more week, and I'd be out of there for good. The personnel manager approached me the next day, stating that the recreation city soccer league, of which I was a volunteer coach, might not "make" for the fall. A search for more coaches had been unsuccessful. Immediately I considered the administrative manager of the warehouse. Why, he's single, loves kids, and has plenty of time!! The league did indeed play, and the gentleman agreed to be a head coach! I heralded a hearty good-bye to all my co-workers and headed straight back to second grade.

October. Stormy weather woke us up early; leaves were playing tag across the field, bidding the lightning to "Catch me if you can". Oh, what a nasty mess. Letting my two boys out at middle school, I asked if they would inform the office to announce that Rotary soccer practice that afternoon would be cancelled. By noon the blue autumn sky had scared off the clouds, and the cool fall day inebriated our spirits.

Same day. 8:30 p.m. Phone jingled. "Hello, of course I remember you (my supervisor for two summers-the coach). No, I did not cancel your soccer practice, I cancelled mine. Oh, me, I didn't realize that Ripley Rotary had two teams. I am so sorry. (Good gracious, how can I make up for this boo-boo? I know...sate a man, save your skin.) We grill burgers and picnic on Saturday nights. How about joining us?" The coach kicked the ball with the kids and even grilled the burgers. Toward the end of the evening he asked my three children out on a "date", stating that it would give me a quiet night...or I was welcome to join them. He relayed later that he was actually feeling sorry for us, for he knew that we probably never had the luxury of dining out. Are you kidding? Me hand my children over to you? I don't think so.

One elegant restaurant. Three grateful kids...well-mannered, too! Seeing eyes agape with wonder, as we four were treated to seafood over-looking the Mississippi River, it was as if Santa had made a delivery two months too soon.

January. Another stormy day about to turn into another elegant affair. In fact, the middle school was broadcasting the local radio warning. I was called to the office about one of my students. Enter the coach into the second grade room, carrying roses, fellow teachers following his invitation to join him. Upon my room re-entrance 24 students cheered, as I spied a diamond dangling from a rose stem. "Will you marry me?" The room was clapping wildly; the children jumped up, asking, "Can we come?" The newspaper photographer snapped pictures, and the radio broadcast the announcement on the news as my boys listened between weather reports! The radio announced proclaimed, "She said, 'Yes'."

Back to Ruth and her "House of Bread" in Bethlehem. Ruth volunteered to glean the fields for food; in Leviticus 23 and

Deuteronomy 24 farmers were instructed to leave some grain for the needy to come and retrieve. Ruth unintentionally went to the field of Boaz, a family relative. In those days, a close relative was to redeem a widow by marrying her, and, since Naomi had been forced to sell her land, both Ruth and the land were available to the closest relative. That relative relayed to Boaz that he could not marry Ruth, so he removed his sandal and handed it to Boaz. The closer relative transferred his right to the property to Boaz. Naomi – empty to full; Ruth – widow to wife.

Like Boaz redeemed Ruth, I sensed God redeeming my life through the coach. The sandal was offered; he not only embraced me but three children. God tenderly graced me with a kind gentle man like Boaz. "He rescued me because He delighted in me." Psalm 18:19, NASB. Times have often not been easy, but I am devoted to him because he mirrored Jesus to me. 27 years later he still reaches over and grabs my hand in the middle of the night.

Follow the Shepherd. He gives us everything we need. He provides the richest of food. He leads us down right paths. Even through uncertain valleys, He gives us everything we need.

I can confidently declare these truths now, because of His gifts of hindsight; being able to remember His past deliverances is the key to working the puzzle of life. I could praise Him loudly; after all, it was my wedding day. But the train still travels on parallel tracks. Good and bad. The house still had closets crammed with "stuff". The weeds still needed pulled up by the roots. Garbage still stinks when it is not dumped, for if sin in the heart is ignored or cherished, God cannot draw near.

Because I had been baptized as an infant, and was now joining my husband in another denomination, I realized that I would need to be immersed in order to come alongside him. Wait a minute, I did not sign up for this! Considering this requirement intolerant and narrow-minded, I was a two year old who was not granted her request for candy in the check-out line. The house hot water heater spewed rusty filth all over the laundry room wall. I did go under, albeit with a terrible horrible no-good very bad attitude. But I was renamed Baptist. And the coach was now dubbed "Jack" by the boys, my daddy's name.

Attending a ladies' Sunday morning Bible class, I heard stories that were unknown to me, only because I had always been a Sunday only Christian. When the girls prayed, their requests were very specific. No "bless the little children" or "forgive us where we fail Thee" but vulnerability and unction. How ridiculous I had considered the coach's childhood story of his family gathered in his den, praying over a broken stove. Surely God doesn't want bothered by such triviality. Why would one bother Him with frivolous things that you could see about yourself?

Up unto this very point, the insights and lessons that I have gleaned have all come to me after I became "diligent to present myself approved to God as a workman who doesn't need to be ashamed, handling accurately the word of truth". 2 Timothy 2:15, NASB.

Jack and I were asked to participate in laying the foundation for a new couples Sunday School class. At the first gathering, the teacher asked that each of us be prepared to share our TESTIMONY. What? Presbyterians don't use that word. How do you get this story? The fact that our Abba is a personal God, that He created us in our mother's womb for a grand purpose, that circumstances were related to His dealing with men...all this was a foreign language, one that even used different symbols for letters. My heart raced to my throat. My breathing became shallow. It was the old familiar panic attack, returning to haunt my days all over again. I've got to get out of here. Run for your life. The Indians are closing in, close on the cowboy's spurs. The rattler is hissing, admonishing your presence. The capsized raft has left the swimmer in a whirlpool,

Qaneh has weathered the hurricane, but her siding dangles, her window panes roost in blades of weeds, and her shingles have soared to Oz. God uses the most uncomfortable methods to get our attention. Good and bad. Panic and calm. Termination or destination. Pride or humility. The straight highway or the road less-traveled.

Choices. Daily minute decisions and life-altering immense determination. The mouse in the house or the termites in the basement: both are daunting to deal with. Earthquakes shake the foundation. "There is an appointed time for everything. And there is a time for every event under heaven...a time to plant and a time to uproot what is planted...a time to tear down and a time to build up...a time to weep and a time to laugh...a time to mourn and a time to dance...a time to embrace and a time to shun embracing." Ecclesiastes 3: 1-5, NASB.

It's a time to settle, no lookin' back. Determine the course of action. No more vacillating. Just as "I do" was recited to the coach, "I will" was whispered to God. It happens in a second, but the repercussions are eternal. "This command I give to you today is not too difficult for you, nor is it out of reach. It is not in heaven.... Nor is it beyond the sea... but the word is very near you, in your mouth and in your heart, that you may observe it. See! I have set before you today life and prosperity, and death and adversity; in that I command you today to love the Lord your God, to walk in His ways and to keep His commandments.... that you may live and multiply, and that the Lord your God may bless you in the land where you are entering to possess it. But, if your heart turns away and you will not obey...I declare to you today that you shall surely perish.... I have set before you life and death, the blessing and the curse. So choose life in order that you and may live, you and your descendants, by loving the Lord your God, by obeying His voice, and by holding fast to Him; **for this is your life**." Deuteronomy 30:11-20, NASB.

Lord, I need a testimony – my own personal story of how You choose to work in me and through me. Ready. Set. Go. But I was *not* prepared for the way in which He would opt to answer me!!! Are we ever?

Another school year. My oldest, John, the budding builder, entered high school, while Will, the lanky quiet thinker, sauntered into eighth grade. My blonde little beauty, Blair, daily followed me to second grade.

November 7. Arriving home from school, I noticed Jack's car in the driveway. "What are you doing home so early?" He clasped my elbow, leading me into the kitchen. "I lost my job today. The plant was bought out, and the managers were lassoed first. My desk has been cleared out, and I'm out."

Covered by His feathers, my normal reaction to fight by fleeing was completely tamed. Another puzzle piece. November led to a cold winter, no job leads, and the severance money was almost depleted. Stoke up the fire; Qaneh's walls are dank and drafty. Cover up with Grandma's quilts and brace yourself against winter's winds.

Exciting news! We are expecting!! But Daddy has no job. Moab or the Promised Land. Sometimes He makes a road in the wilderness only to lead us to an oasis. February teased with a few warm days, a few job leads, but don't move the coats to the attic yet.

March 7....the perfect number! During math class, I noticed Jack's face pressed against the glass. "I've been offered a job! They want me to start next week!" Oh, hallelujah, Lord! "Jill, it's in Asheville, North Carolina." I am 38 years old, been livin' in west Tennessee all my life, my family is here, a baby's on the way. My children?

Dance or mourn. God's will or a test? Trust and obey or doubt and rebel. Break the children's spirits or open opportunity's doors. I am the Velveteen Rabbit becoming REAL. "It doesn't happen to people who break easily, or have sharp edges, or who have to be carefully kept. But the time you are REAL, most of your hair has been loved off, your eyes drop out, and you get loose in the joints and very shabby."[7]

Choices. I humbly admit that my 'yes' was more for me and less for the significant issues my children would face. Acting a bit (no, a lot) like Emililech, I was ready to run from the scare of being so long without a steady paycheck. And, of all the places He could have desired for us, He chose to grace us with the paradise of Eden itself. A mountain home, constructed when my grandmother Baba was only a toddler, a stream meandering through the backyard, three acres of quiet beauty!

Looking back over the last 27 years, I see His fingerprints all over my life. But divorce and remarriage and a major move and step-siblings...if I gaze too intently in that mysterious arena, it causes aches deep in the folded recesses of my soul. All on the altar I lay only to alter their sweet lives into a vortex of vacillating circumstances beyond their control? Do any of us really have control over any issue though? Dependence on God or independence. Even freedom isn't free. Even self-made wealthy money-grabbing entrepreneurs are pawns in His hand. To be or not to be? That is the question for us all.

3

Rock-A-Bye Baby

March 7. Jack was living in an Asheville motel while I finished the school year. It was a Saturday afternoon. Will, Blair, her friend Natalie, and I decided to travel fifteen miles to visit my mother. Darkness marched its way forward, so we loaded up the car to return home. Pulling out onto her street, I realized that I'd forgotten some pictures I had shared with her, so we returned to retrieve them. Another few minutes of conversation, and we were on our way. Approaching the bridge (the same one that I had used as a pivot-point to make it half-way during panic attack days), I saw a man wildly waving his hands. "Stop. Bridge is out." As I recall, seven people lost their lives that day, tumbling head-first into the swollen muddy Hatchie River. The pictures I had forgotten. My first small story! God's ways are not man's ways, beyond our comprehension, but, HE SAVED me, my two children, another family's child, and my unborn baby. I grieved for those lost and have prayed that their families have seen Him somehow through their barren times.

Still March. Being called to the school office for a phone call was unusual. The nurse from the obstetrician's office was on the line. "Could you come in for more tests? The lab work shows your baby might possibly have spinal bifida...or it could be twins." Such a cold delivery. My hot heart raced. No one to run to. Nowhere to go. Yes, there was One. My husband was gone. Just return to the classroom and carry on? Alone and crushed...I cried myself to sleep. Jack came home for an amniocyntesis; I was carrying a healthy baby boy.

May. The 16 year old builder boy announced, "I am not going with you! I have school, friends, a job, and a girlfriend. No way."

May's end. The children's father appeared at my door. "Will wants to stay; he's 14, can decide for himself, and no court would agree to let you take him 465 miles from what he's known."

Is this a pay-back for my decision six years ago, to agree to allow them to live with their dad? God, do You keep score? Is it true what the radio preacher said... that the greatest opportunities in life come disguised as totally unsolvable problems? Lord, You have re-enrolled me in a course that I never signed up for the first time. Why, they are still children...and another due in ten days.

Hannah prayed so unctuously for her womb to be opened. Her husband, Elkanah, begged her to eat and drink. "Why is your heart so sad?" But Eli, the priest surmised that she had had too much to drink. "Put away your wine." His hasty criticism only strove to censure her devotion to a Savior she trusted. God appreciated Hannah's respectful candor. She poured out her heart in very specific requests to her Savior and left her basket of cares at His feet. "She went her way and her face was no longer sad." 1 Samuel 1:18, NASB.

Before His answer came! Her countenance was changed! How often I lay my basket down at the foot of the Cross but then run back to only pick it up again and clutch it closely. Hannah, how could you desire a baby so much that you would give him up as soon as he was weaned? Hand him over to another to care for? God is asking me to do just that, and it's ripping my heart out. You are more of a woman than I will ever be. Jochebed, how did you ever have the courage and trust to place your baby, the one who kicked inside of you, the wee one you cradled in your arms and sang lullabies to, the one who smelled of heaven itself, into a tar-pitched basket on a swollen muddy mighty riverbank? **Lord, I am not through loving them.** Must I be asked to wave "good bye" only days before my swollen belly gives birth to what they surely must perceive is their "replacement"? Will I have to offer this little boy up, like I've done with all the others?

Randy Pausch in his book *The Last Lecture* gave a profound interpretation of what, on the surface, seem to be disastrous occurrences. "Experience is what you get when you didn't get what you wanted. And it's the most valuable thing you have to offer. Failure is not just acceptable, it's essential."[8] Experience *is* valuable, but Jesus wins. Wisdom is the perfect result gained from experience: "My son, *if* you accept my (wisdom's) words and store up my commandments within you, listening closely and directing your heart to understanding; *if* you call out to insight and lift your voice to understanding, *if* you seek it like silver and search for it like hidden treasure, *then* you *will* understand the fear of the Lord and discover the knowledge of God...He stores up success for the upright; He is a shield for those who live with integrity, ...You *will* understand righteousness, justice, and integrity-every good path. Wisdom *will* enter your mind, and knowledge *will* delight your heart." Proverbs 2: 1-9, HCSB, emphasis mine. Let's Make a Deal: a win-win situation. What glorious promises!

Every baby boy has been "clothed with skin and flesh and knit together with bones and sinews and been granted life and favor." Job 10:11, NKJ. "The Spirit of God has made me, and the breath of the Almighty gives me life." Job 33:4, NKJ. "For it was You who created my inward parts; You knit me together in my mother's womb. I will praise You, because I have been remarkably and wonderfully made. Your works are wonderful, and I know this very well. My bones were not hidden from You when I was made in secret, and formed in the depths of the earth. Your eyes saw me when I was formless; all my days were written in Your book and planned before a single one of them began." Psalm 139:13-16, NASB.

John and Will were never promised to me to hold onto for a lifetime. A fretful spirit and analyzed afflictions in a worldly heart are our own worst enemies. God could have been a grand comfort to me if I had run to Him and jumped up in His lap, but His comfort was elusive. Rejoice or mourn. Laugh or cry. Hasten to Him or DIY. Speaking of the Jews' deliverance from Egypt, Matthew Henry disclosed, "They bore the miseries of their servitude better than the difficulties of their deliverance."[9]

Memorial Day weekend. I flew to Asheville and we bought a house.

First of June. What was the sheriff doing in my driveway? Serving me papers, issuing a restraining order. I was not to take Will (high school freshman) out of the state of Tennessee.

June 14. Wednesday. Movers at my backdoor to box up our hay, wood, and stubble.

June 15. Thursday. A one hour trip to the Memphis airport to greet Jack. We requested that the restraining order be rescinded.

June 16. Friday. Moving van loaded. Do we send Will's belongings ahead as an act of faith? Or will God in His mysterious ways keep this Tennessee boy in Rocky Top?

June 16. Friday. 9:00p.m. Taylor was born into all our chaos. The bizarre blueprints given to Mary and Joseph couldn't have been drawn up by any fleshly architect. Fabricating the framing on such a permanent estate could only be manufactured by a Master Designer. But because of the flawless measurements which He had laid out, the cornerstone was sure to be square and give strength to the erected walls. Doesn't His Word say the same about each of our individual circumspections? "Humble yourselves under the mighty hand of God, that He might exalt you at the proper time, casting all your anxiety on Him, **because He cares for you.**" I Peter 5:6-7, NASB.

Sometimes we could care less about the exaltation part, we just need a rope to hang onto. "Two are better than one because they have a good return for their labor. If either of them falls, the one will lift up his companion. But woe to the one who falls when there is not another to lift him up....A cord of three strands is not easily broken." Ecclesiastes 4:9,10,12, NASB. Just hang on to me, Lord, just hang on a little while longer.

Because he was a new employee and had already missed three work days, Jack drove us to my mother's house on Sunday morning, loaded up Blair and Chelsea, our Springer spaniel, and headed off for the mountains. Will, Taylor, and I were to fly to Knoxville (Jack's parents) on Thursday and wait for the judge's decision. We waited...waited...and waited some more, not being able to cross the North Carolina line. At three minutes before the courthouse closed on Friday afternoon, we received a call allowing us temporarily to go "home". But the 16 year old builder boy still hammered his nails in west Tennessee. "Oh, El Shaddai, care for Him."

New job. New baby. A son left behind. Another wishing he had been. A third grader caught in the mire. An old farmhouse that begged for repairs. An eight hour ride back to Tennessee in two weeks to face the dentist. God's loving plan or a huge misunderstanding. But what an experience we were gaining! And this would only be the beginning.

The court allowed Will to become a Tar Heel. Parallel tracks. Good and bad.

4

Wee Willie Winkie

Bless this house, O Lord, we pray; make it safe by night and day. What keeps the sagging roof from caving in? What holds up the porch? The invisible bones strain to give the surface a well-kept appearance. Vines and mildew and termites eat away at the siding. Qaneh's proud façade keeps on keepin' on. More than DIY is needed to strip away her problems.

The North Carolina farmhouse showered many marvelous memories...the mountain creek in the backyard, the old massive maple tree that shed its gorgeous fall leaves, the tractor rides around our three acres, the dog scratching at our open bedroom window at eleven p.m. nightly, picnics on mountaintops, the porch swing lulling a baby to sleep. The mountains grabbed my soul; their beauty brought God's presence. Leaving family, friends, and familiarity, as difficult as it was, faded into the backdrop; my Tennessee testimony prayer request seemed to be writing a story in my heart. Swing the baby, sing praises, see what God has prepared for those who wait on Him. And our hearts found a home church filled with caring, lovely disciples. Witness this promise: "The Lord is near to the broken-hearted, and He saves those who are crushed in spirit. Many adversities come to the one who is righteous, but the Lord delivers him *from them all."* Psalm 34: 18-19, HCSB. Not *out of* the trial but straight through the middle!

Our faith began to blossom, especially by the touch of Fred and Ann Vernon. From the first Sunday that Ann saw our three week old Taylor enter the nursery, he was all hers. She often laughed that I had brought him in from a nap, clad in only a diaper. Oh, that we would come to Jesus stripped of our rags. She became my mama away from home. We all named them Grandpa and Grandma.

She was there the winter's day that the trees were wholly bare of their garments. Fall had been extremely cumbersome for Will; a strange new high school in which he knew no one was a giant much too foreboding to slay with only five small stones. My compliant son was not adapting well to all the newness; he wouldn't, or couldn't, eat, so his tall lanky frame grew even frailer. In the pre-dawn hours of that last Advent Sunday morning, I headed to the kitchen for sustenance for my crying baby only to view another starving son's cry: "Mom, please let me go back to my friends." This was 24 years ago, but my heart is still freshly pierced by its pleading. The ashes of hostility that lingered for the dentist were stoked into a raging fire. Standing in the kitchen doorway spewing and stewing like a hungry dragon, the Lord's words stopped me cold: "Is this how Jesus would have reacted?"

"Well, Lord, I'm not sure. I have a right..."

"He gave His up. See for yourself."

Three days after Christmas, the car, loaded with his belongings and my grieving heart, headed down I-40 westward to meet his father at a half-way point. Now I knew just a fraction of the wretchedness, of the ravaged suffering of the Father as He gave up His Son for us. It is not who wins or who loses. We would all win if we would just choose Jesus. His death that looked so bad to His own became the most glorious Sunday morning that ever dawned.

So I did began to see for myself, to search the Scriptures with all my mind and strength, seeking every tidbit that was related to the words vengeance, revenge, repayment, retribution, reparation, requital, and forgiveness. I was *not* disappointed! Also, because I was at home, the radio waves became my new best friend. All through-out the day I soaked up messages from humble men of God and was absolutely blown away by mysteries unknown to me. Thirty-eight years old, still drinking milk like a babe.

"Strength and dignity are her clothing, and she smiles at the future." Proverbs 31: 25, NASB. "When you cannot hear God, you will find that He has trusted you in the most intimate way possible, for He saw that you could withstand an even bigger revelation. As long as you have the idea that God will always bless you in answer to prayer, He will do it, but He will never give you the grace of His silence. The first sign of His intimacy is silence."[10]

Like a child giggling with delight as he catches floating bubbles, I was running around reaching for His truths, afraid one would pop before it would be cemented in my soul. The pages in my Bible became dog-eared and marked with tears of thanksgiving and wisdom. "Really? How cool is that!" Another promise: "You will make known to me the path of life; in Your presence is fullness of joy!" Psalm 16:11, NASB.

He took these chains off so I could cha-cha. Just as Abraham was justified (just as if he had never sinned) by his faith, obedience to the faith he proclaimed was the next necessary step. "You see, his faith was active together with his works, and by works, faith was perfected. So the Scripture (Old Testament) was fulfilled that says, 'Abraham believed God, and it was credited to him for righteousness, and He was called God's friend. You see that a man is justified by works and not by faith alone." James 2:21-24, HCSB. He laid his son Isaac on the altar, not asking for God's explanation, with the full intention of slaying the heir to God's promise.

Tony Evans, pastor of Oak Cliff Bible Church, relayed that unforgiveness is "like drinking poison and waiting for the other person to die". "When one slings mud, he loses a lot of ground and only gets dirty himself."

Making a list of Scriptures dealing with revenge, I had come up with over twenty. No, Jesus and I were not on the same page. The place I was sitting, a blue leather chair and ottoman, wrapped in a blue and white lap blanket and peering out at his mountains, when I discovered Matthew 5:23-24 (NASB), snapped a Polaroid moment that no camera could ever delete. "If, therefore, you are presenting your offering at the altar, and there remember that your brother has something against you, leave your offering there before the altar, and go your way; first be reconciled to your brother and then come and present your offering." No matter what the dentist's reaction, which is not your responsibility, GO. No more playing the deadly game, "If only..."

Out came the note paper and pen. "Please know that I ask you to forgive me for any action on my part, but, from this day forward there will be no more wrestling with you. I mourn that the boys' young years have been so tense in *our* tug-of-war game. Childhood and innocence are a hand and glove and should be carefree and sweet, but we two have stolen their candy. The next three years will not be easy, but *you* will get to finish what *I* should have been there to experience. If you choose not to send any child support for Blair, we will make it just fine."

"We pour out our miseries, God just hears a melody. The honest cries of a breaking heart are better than a 'Hallelujah' sometime."[11] God's smile washed all over me the day I traipsed the long gravel driveway and raised the red mailbox flag. The whole bloody scenario washed as clean as the new fallen snow.

5

Along Came a Spider

Almost three years in Asheville. My man was working lengthy hours. I would see his headlights wind down the drive, but he would linger in the dark truck. His work environment was causing great tension. Being an early-morning person and a long-range planner did not blend with a late-afternoon go-getter supervisor, who thrived when working in last minute chaos. Labor that could have been taken care of in the morning hours was put on the front burner as urgent at 4:00 p.m. So, when a church friend approached him about initiating a business venture that had grown too fast for him to steer alone, Jack began to study his options.

Ron, a chemical engineer, wanted to oversee product production as Jack took care of the business/public relations end. Contracts and prospects appeared to be all in fine array, so, partly fearing for his health, I joined him in support of his new adventure, for Ron had given a winning testimony about God's faithfulness on Sunday night at church. An ad campaign was commenced, which included TV commercials. Of course, business start-ups require a chunk of money; $17,000 was borrowed to launch the enterprise. My man was animated again; he was created for challenge and for conquering the vast frontier. Several months passed, all promising prosperity. Jack jaunted down to the warehouse one morning, and, as the overhead door disappeared into the garret, he was struck dumb. The belly of the warehouse had vomited out every barrel of manufactured product. Empty. Not even a mouse. Squeaky clean but disgustingly trashed. Ron was nowhere to be found. Vanished into unknown spaces. Where does one go from here? And...I was pregnant again.

God's prophet Jeremiah was thrown into prison by his *own* people for proclaiming that God was about to judge them for their detestable idol worship and gross ungodly actions. Their ears wanted to be tickled to glad tidings, not the truth. (Familiar, huh?) While Jeremiah was shut up in a dingy dungeon, two visitors came calling. The first was a heavenly one: the Lord explained that he would have a second visitor, his cousin. How unusual! Jeremiah was an outcast – utterly isolated. No one visited a derelict, especially to make a request such as this one: His uncle Shallum was experiencing hardships and needed to sell some land. Would Jeremiah consider redeeming it? Sell farm land to a convict? And to top this tale off, this field was no longer family property; the acreage was currently spoil for the Babylonians, who were plundering Jerusalem!

We were in a prison as surely as Jeremiah. The jail cell in which our souls were shackled seemed every bit as real. No job. New baby. In debt. House for sale. Septic tank backed up. Just as Qaneh is surrounded by broken windows, discarded yard trash, and succulent vines that have attached their hungry claws even to hollow places, our lives had been T-boned.

It would be only in hindsight, many paces down a worn path, that the lesson would be learned. God allowed Babylon to overcome His own people – for a season. But, when we can't see His hand, we *can* know His heart. He foreordained that the Jews would be captives in a foreign land for seventy years, a wilderness experience just like the first one. For forty years Moses had led a stiff-necked stubborn people, as they wandered in a desert of confusion and frustration. It didn't *have* to be that way. Though we are smack in the middle of defeat, if we look to Him in sorrow over our rebellion, and seek His face, He *will* restore us.

The **test** wasn't for the Jews alone but for His messenger. God **tested** Jeremiah: "Do you really believe what you preach? Then buy the land. If it isn't worth investing in, it isn't worth believing in." God *will* test the reality of our faith; this is the real blessing! "All that is untried is not faith!"[12]

FAITH: Forsaking All I Trust Him.

"Let no one say when he is tempted, 'I am being tempted by God'; for God cannot be tempted by evil, and He Himself does not tempt anyone. But each one is being tempted when he is carried away and lured by his own lust." James 1:13-14, NASB. Temptation and Test are not synonymous. God tests for our good to increase our faith. Satan tempts us to drag us into the pit, but our own fleshly worldly desires also allure us into biting perilous bait. Sin takes one further than he wants to go and costs more than one is willing to pay.

This is why I write. We need to share. We need spiritual mamas and daddies. We need vulnerability. We need mentors, and mentors need us. I did not know at the time that what was happening was a blessing from His hand. He'd been up all night preparing a table for me. He was anointing my head with oil. Not only did I not respond to His sweet invitation, I never showed up for the party, never brought Him a present of praise; I even spurned His kindness. "Surely goodness and mercy will follow me all the days of my life." Psalm 23:6, NASB. "Ah, Lord God, You have made the heavens and the earth by Your great power and outstretched arm! Nothing is too difficult for you!" Jeremiah 32:17, NASB.

Doubt can destroy, devastate, or dictate deliverance. "God, why is this happening to me?" We can publish our anguish, but it is very contagious. We can keep it bottled up, but boiling turmoil under wrap causes the cork to blow at some point. We can take it to the Lord by being transparent and honest; He can handle it! "When all circumstances on the outside are crumbling walls of defeat, the feelings on the inside can be a glassy sea of serenity."[13] The school of hard knocks is led by a tough-love task-master, but how prudent we are when we graduate.

Jeremiah 32:17-25 relays Jeremiah's beautiful response to God's bidding – before the answer had come. The priests put their feet in the swollen Jordan River to lead the way to Jericho, the first stop in the Promised Land, only because Abba had promised, that, if they would rest after getting their feet muddy, that they would witness His power divide the overflowing river. The golden ark, carrying the manna, Aaron's rod, and the commandments led the way, poised on the priests' shoulders. Jesus is our ark of safety; enter His rest *before* He shows up to deliver. Alertness. Courage. Obedience. Confidence. Deliverance. In order.

God will, in the fullness of His time, send confirmation and reassurance. Grab hold of that three-stranded cord and hang on 'til you feel underneath the everlasting arms. God promised Jeremiah that the Jews would come home. *"I will* put My law in their minds and write it on their hearts; *I will* be their God, and they *shall be* My people.... They all *shall know* (*personally, intimately*) Me."* Jeremiah 31:31-34, NKJ, emphasis mine.

Although Jeremiah bought the land without seeing it, he believed this was a pledge of restoration, for Abba had promised to make an everlasting covenant with them to never turn away again. Jesus, the Vine who gives the branches eternal life, was the answer to Abba's promise; ultimately, in the New Jerusalem, heaven itself, we will dance and sing and thank Him for throwing such a glorious party.

Creditors called. Cabinets cleared. Banks are only so patient for a season. How do we handle this renegade absconder? Who will deliver a baby without recompense? I felt Mary's pain and fright as she traveled alone with Joseph to Bethlehem. The time for delivery was nigh. Sitting at the health office among a sea of humanity allowed me to learn humility. Grandma and Grandpa were there to love on us and to tend to the children.

In December, two months before our last son was to arrive, we made a trek to Tennessee to witness my first-born recite his wedding vows. John was only eighteen and still had a semester of high school. I was seven months pregnant, and my son would become a dad himself on the heels of Pomp and Circumstance.

Our son made his appearance right at suppertime! The cold February night delivered the warmth of holding this fresh gift from heaven. A Valentine blessing right when we needed it most! As fingers and toes were counted and tender kisses exchanged, this mama and daddy observed what appeared to be a large birthmark across Walker's back. "We are not sure what we are dealing with yet," were the doctor's words, but words inside my head were clear: "It will go away!" Walker was surrounded by a bevy of onlookers and med students, wanting a look at this unusual marking; the blackness was as an open envelope which wrapped around both sides of his body, covered his back across the top of his buttocks and made a point directly between the lower range of his shoulder blades. I remember a remark, "It appears to be a nevus (mole); we would like to send him to a children's hospital in Greenville, SC, for a biopsy." His birth date was Monday (Monday's child is fair of face); the next Sunday morning we presented him to the church congregation, asking for fervent prayers.

A home-made altar was perched on our kitchen table, made from twelve stones collected in our yard. Altar: an elevated holy table. When Noah had been delivered from the flood, he built the first altar and offered sacrifices to God as an act of worship. Noah had obeyed God's request to build the ark; even as onlookers jeered and joked, Noah day by day continued his project exactly as he was directed.

I counted seventeen altars in the Old Testament; my son was born on the seventeenth. At the altar, one declared open confession of God, worshiped Him there, and asserted faith that God would accept his sacrifice and act on his behalf for His glory. This was our open confession: we believe You; we trust You. A small sign was created and folded as our banner, words from Joshua as the swollen Jordan River subsided and the Jews were deposited safely in Canaan, the Promise Land. "When your children ask their fathers in time to come, saying, 'What are these stones?', then you shall let your children know, saying, 'Israel crossed over this Jordan (River) on dry land...as He did to the Red Sea... that all the peoples of the earth might *know (intimately)* the hand of the Lord, that it is mighty, that you may fear the Lord your God forever'." Joshua 4:21-24, NKJ, emphasis mine.

My newly-wed prayer for a testimony remained in its infancy, but it had been born.

5:00 a.m. February 24, Walker's one week birthday. We were en route to South Carolina with a fussy unfed newborn for surgery at 8:00 a.m. On arrival we were told there would be a two hour delay. Our eight-pounder had had no nourishment since midnight...toooo long. Whimpers became screams. Unrest became torture. Ripples of calmness became torrential tsunamis. The pacifier offered no healing balm. Heart surgery had already cut into my tender soul as I sat helpless. "O Jerusalem, Jerusalem... how often I have wanted to gather your children together as a hen gathers her chicks under her wings, but you were not willing." Matthew 23:37, NKJ. I felt Jesus' pain.

He could have demanded obedience, but Love is a Perfect Gentleman. Love must be set free; how blessedly magnificent it is when it returns. But I was a helpless mess, a pool of melting magma. Handing my baby over to a stranger....oh, my, like raw sewage in a flooded river basin, my tears spill all over again. How did my Father willingly surrender His Son for me? It was so simple to gaze on the kitchen altar and promise to lay my all on the altar. But, when hot wilderness winds smack in the face with biting sand, can I, will I, still trustfully echo those same words? Peter reverberated, "Lord, to whom shall we go?" John 6:68, NKJ. And that's the truth. To whom else is there? Bitter or better; that's the choice.

The biopsy result returned: non-cancerous nevi. But even if it hadn't, I know I would have still have hung onto the hem of His garment. We still would face fifteen more surgeries. Arriving home we collected two anxious children; we didn't realize that that very day we would receive our last hug from Grandpa. One new life, one gone.

Five weeks later we once again handed our little one over to the care of strangers. The surgeon performed dermabrasion on one-third of the entire mole. Removing the top three of seven layers of skin and then then covering it with a yellow waxy gauze, we were instructed that it would molt as he healed.

Walker developed a low-grade fever; the doctor was called, who surmised that it was "just a bug." Amidst our concern, we threw a birthday bash for Grandma. After supper, she attended to Walker. As she turned around, there was a grim announcement: "This must come off!" We not only had a nursemaid but a nurse. The mustard bandage had adhered to the wound as the vine has to Qaneh. Like a child planting his foot in a rebellious temper tantrum, this healing balm had turned traitor. Tentacles of a vine do not appreciate the landscaper's discipline, nor was the stubborn bandage going to cede victory without heated combat. Glancing at the corner as it began to be pulled away, crimson blood beads began to bubble. I turned my head and fled, not able to view his torture. I could hear Mary's wail at the foot of the cross. Although just a blood-drop in the bucket of His sacrifice, this was no less a mother's frightening nightmare at the moment.

In my naivety, I surmised that the wound would now begin to heal. Clad only in a diaper, he lay quietly on my chest, then Jack's, then mine, Friday night through Saturday. He grew fussy and the fever continued; another call was made. Greenville was several hours away, and we were asked to take him to emergency. We began calling doctors in town. Medicaid plus joblessness equals engulfing embarrassment. No one would take us in; fixing someone else's problem was risky.

By Monday morning he was on the altar of grace. My pediatrician could not practice at the hospital! Somebody, please care! We showed up at the hospital, not knowing if the innkeeper would take us in. He was immediately admitted. Seeing that tiny body in that metal cage all hooked up to wires was another parallel track: hope going toward one destination, gloom in the other. We were told it was possibly blood poisoning and that he would require massive antibiotics. We stood over him as sentries: watching, guarding, straining to view even a hint of relief wave across his face, as his tiny body was cradled and dipped below the bubbling balm of a miniature whirlpool. Bathed three times daily, laid on his tummy on a warm soft blanket, Walker (and Mama and Daddy) were cradled in the feathers of Abba's wing. As each little piece of loosened scab was tediously tweezed away, our pacifier was a tasty treasure of security.

Looking in the rear-view mirror, my unctuous prayer for a testimony, His-story in me, was being worked out just as He purposed. Work one piece at a time. A little here, a little there. Isaiah 28:10b, NASB. A little lesson here, a little lesson there. Enlighten the mind to win His affection, bring the will into compliance with His commands, then He comes in the door of the heart...if we but heed the still small Voice. Don't you know that that is how He deals with His children? He never sleeps, He stands guard over us, all the while waiting to be the Recipient of our "ah-ha" moments and our praises. Deliberately, patiently, He picks away the scabs of sin, softened by grace and tenderness. Pick. Pick. Pick. He lovingly and gently trashes my black, unsightly, crusty sin in the pool of Siloam. The harshness has already been dealt with, my punishment was laid on His Son in the three hours of blackness, a darkness that was gloriously crying, then cooing, overcome by the light of the Resurrection morn! Pain turned to peace.

Just like Qaneh in her fractured brokenness, in the house of Syria there lived a jaded army commander. Unlike Qaneh, however, the dilapidation wasn't external, but internal; even though his leprosy was visible and unsightly, Naaman's heart was fatigued. Israel and Syria had never dined at the same table. But Providence led this rich, honorable, mighty man of valor to seek aid from an unlikely place, for under his table a tasty crumb had fallen that would permanently nourish the soul.

In one of Naaman's victories over Israel, he had captured a young Jewish girl, who ultimately was used in his deliverance. Under his regal uniform lay sickly festering blemishes. This maid, unwillingly taken captive, had agreeably diffused the knowledge of God by conveying to her captor a cure for his diseased body. Tidings of joy brought by a strange happenstance? How could this child-suffering wilderness bring forth a Rose into our lives? Flowers do not bloom in the sand! Yet we are here, holding our new-born's clasped hand around our fingers as we allow healing to come through odd events.

Naaman's cure came through a prophet's message: He should wash himself in the muddy Jordan River seven times. God's number of perfection! But there were two magnificent rivers in Damascus. Why this less-traveled way? Too cheap. Too plain. Too common. Would he, could he, should he just obey a simple incongruous message? Will I? Naaman became as a little child, humbled himself, by listening to his inferior servant's advice, and scaly scabs became as an infant's baby smooth skin. The Great Physician had tenderly tweezed every rough ulcerated nodule, and Naaman skipped twenty-five miles back to Elijah's house to pay the prophet for his advice, but the wealth of the world was garbage to Elijah. Wash and be clean. Believe and be saved. Repent and be pardoned. Impressed by the cure or affected by the Miracle-giver?

Five days of warm dips in the pool of Siloam ("conductor")[14]. Just as Jerusalem's inhabitants were refreshed by water piped in from an underground spring, we were invigorated by His care through church members who became His hands and feet. We saw Jesus through outstretched hands and fervent prayers. We went home, and the five of us gathered around the homemade rock altar, thanking Him for His love. Without Will. With no job, a mortgage, and an empty cabinet. But deliverance **had** shown up! And I *began* to be cemented in the belief that He would be faithful...no matter what.

It was a sweet tradition on Friday nights to pull out the sofa bed, pop popcorn, and all pile in and watch sitcoms. Our Chelsea, a Springer spaniel, would slither under the metal bed frame and enjoy the fellowship, too. One Friday night, Taylor, three years old, wallowed under the bed to see his buddy. He exclaimed, "Sumpthins comin' out of Chesee!" To our amazement, a small new creature, fresh from Abba's hands, greeted us with closed eyes but sent an open message of love and life. After scooting her to a soft bed in the kitchen corner, she birthed four more soft furry wee creatures! Watching our dog care for her brood was a day at the county fair, a ferris wheel of delight, lifted high above the muck and mire of the dust and the animal refuse.

Mortgage late notices became frequent. Resumes were in the mail but went unheeded. I particularly remember one creditor calling, asking why we charged our gasoline if we were unable to pay the bill. A $17,000.00 business loan still had Jack's name on it, even though the business was ka-put. He was offered a job roofing houses, earning $8.00 an hour, and I opened my home to two babies, another Will and Derrick (Deke-Deke to Taylor). This would at least give us grocery money.

The mountains in spring sent beauty and a freshness that winter had suppressed. But the $600.00 house note was a mighty battle to wage. We were never on time and never supplied the full amount. And the $17,000.....well, a judgment was issued against us. Treading water, we were being pulled down into a dirty muddy cesspool. Outside our back door even our septic tank malfunctioned. Again. A white banner of surrender whispered defeat in our ears and echoed noxious notions through its smell. It is only through raging rivers that we desire to seek higher ground. Rising waters threaten to undo us, but the winds of Love blow on.

Take note, though, we did *not* advertise our circumstances. Just the opposite, it was embarrassing. 465 miles from "home", but God had us exactly where He wanted us. He always does, unless we kick against the goads. Only in the wilderness can one find an oasis. No family to rely on, but the mountain stream in our back yard flowed cool and clear. No money, but poverty has a way of rescuing the soul from the pursuit of the trivial. Don't number the minutes, for they will stop time dead.

Delivery arrived in an assortment of flavors and colors.

May 26. Our new granddaughter Alyssa made her debut. When I was teaching, I thought it odd, even eccentric, that a few of my students over the years had aunts and uncles who were contemporaries. Now I was the targeted bulls-eye. Walker was an uncle at three months of age!

Multi-faceted holy trials often splotch themselves all over us, like a near-empty bottle of mustard left upside down, whose contents explode as the cap is hurriedly popped open. But Jesus' loving plans have purposed each projectile to hit its target: bull's eye every time! The postman wended his way down the curved gravel driveway and honked his horn. A card arrived, which needed my signature. A strange way to birth liberation, but isn't that God's norm? Keep your eyes open, ears attentive to His whisper, hands completely unclasped, and expect the unexpected. A green colored envelope from Pleasant Hill Baptist Church in Lenoir City, Tennessee. What a sweet gesture for Jack's dad's church to encourage us. But how did they know? Tucked inside was an extremely generous love gift.

My dear friend from west Tennessee came for a mountain visit. After her loyalty and love through the divorce, the ties that bound us drew even tighter, and I had missed her companionship. The morning I hugged her good-bye, I turned in emptiness to face the lonely day. The dirty dishes washed me in pity. Lying in the kitchen windowsill was a wad of bills. The morning sun rising above the mountain watched me sitting in the kitchen floor wetting the drying towel with my bottled up tears.

During my grocery store run, Jack received a call from our missions pastor. I returned to tears spilling over the veneer that he had pasted on his countenance. Joe relayed how that his prayers had been hindered that morning with Jack's name, so "What did we need?" It gave us an opportunity to humble ourselves, quite not the norm for either of us. The church was overdue for an audit on its books, so Jack was hired to delve into that project. Church friends opened a day care and asked for assistance in setting up books.

Even though puzzle pieces were already laid out in heaven, the Architect was not ready to reveal His final sketches...yet. The house note was still an ogre to be reckoned with; we had robbed Peter to pay Paul for so long that often, as we took one baby step forward, we would stumble backwards two. The old farmhouse was put on the market, but for several months no one bit the bait we cast on the waters.

The bank sent notice that no more partial payments would be accepted. If we couldn't produce the owed money, three months of payments or $1800.00, by the Tuesday after Labor Day, foreclosure procedures would begin. Oh, would someone please love our house? Plopping down Jack's retirement fund from the automotive plant, we had made a down payment of almost $20,000, which would be flushed out into the smelly septic tank area in the back field. Our dilemma, however, did not catch the Father by surprise, for the timing of the symphony of deliverance had been orchestrated in the heavenlies by the master Conductor. Softly a few instruments began to play until the fullness of time; crescendos must await the climax.

Jack's family gathered near-by on Labor Day week-end for his aunt and uncle's fiftieth wedding anniversary. As we climbed in the car for the ninety minute drive home, his sister handed him a sealed envelope with his name on it. Good-byes and hugs given, the seal was broken to reveal $1800.00 cash! There was no name, but a some-body, who chose not to be credited with our rescue, was used to increase our faith walk. This mystery agent mentioned something about wanting to help with expenses for Walker's surgeries. *No one* knew about our house plight...no One but El Shaddai. El is Power; Shad is breast. The Spirit moves to and fro, going wherever He wills. And He willed to come to us at the midnight hour. "Jesus loves me, this I know, for the Bible tells me so." How often we have sung those words, gathered in a circle of wee chairs at Sunday School, but yet the appropriating of His love remains a foreign language, ignored by most until the carriage turns back into a pumpkin after the ball. God almost never shows up early, but He is never late. If I believe the He is who He says He is, without wavering to and fro like the sea waves, even at 11:59 p.m., the candle is still brightly burning in my window bidding Him to enter....and He does.

The bank was reimbursed in full on the first Tuesday in September. The house remained unsold until December 23, but the cold weather prohibited the septic tank from barking its ugly taunting. Christmas was quite a celebration. All five children rested their feet under my table, along with a spouse and a new granddaughter. It did not matter that we knew not where we would be planted soon, but our family was unshackled! Chains were gone; we were set free to love. Our most treasured memories come through the most painful sufferings. Warm sweet fellowship around the table with those we love, hands clasped in thanksgiving, a rock altar centerpiece offering hope: higher plane distinctives always rise above our poverty and overrule Satan's clandestine purposes. Praise is a savory aroma to His nostrils, and He smiles.

6

...They Licked the Platter Clean

From Monte Vista to Vista Drive. Approximately three miles. Worldly possessions were boxed. Again. Ten years since single motherhood had wrapped me in robes of unflattering fabric. Our "new" rental house would be dwelling number seven for me, and it would host a birthday bash for the baby. Even though a path was shoveled through the still-taped boxes, we sang wildly.

February 15. The date our little farmhouse was transferred to another lover. Memories abound. The creek running through the backyard. The mountain-view from the attic bedroom. Cool mountain air rolling down the hills through the window screens. Will sitting on the ledge above the stairs, his long legs dangling. My little boys shedding diapers on the back porch, having contests to see who could tee-tee the farthest distance. The soothing sound of gravel crunching beneath truck tires as I realized my man was home. A wood plank kitchen floor lovingly laid late at night. The front porch swing and how it soothed two crying infants; the fields covering their ears as I sang lullabies. The curtains crafted from blankets bought in Chimney Rock as we meandered narrow winding mountain roads. Sleeping "upside down" at the foot of our bed, so that Jack could catch the cool night air from his side of the bed. The gigantic maple tree strutting brilliant fall colors; giggling youngsters rolling around in the newly fallen leaves. Tractor rides with dad over three acres-until the engine went ker-ploot one day. Late night probing under front bushes seeking the last pacifier. Friday nights piled up with popcorn on the sofa bed. Chelsea's birthing surprise. Parallel tracks running their course. Gracious plenty contented memories run the race with often tedious trials.

A Little Golden book entitled *Tootle the Train* relates the tale of a baby locomotive in training to become a Flyer. Earning A+ in Staying on the Rails No Matter What is vital. But Tootle was tempted to race with Black Beauty, then later to dance with the buttercups, then to chase butterflies, and lastly to create daisy chains. It wasn't until the towns' people all tutored him in Stop for a Red Flag Waving did he stay the course and graduate. Through his wanderings he matured into a Two-Mile-a-Minute Flyer, and it was via the wisdom learned through instruction that he was rewarded as a mentor to other baby locomotives.[15]

When I venture forth to explore my own pleasures and fool myself into thinking, "I'm His, He'll understand", I have been carried away into a meadow of stunning, but poisonous, poppies. Just ask Dorothy and her Oz –bound friends: One sniff of their sweetness leads to a delayed destination. No battle, no victory. No wounds, no battle scars. No wandering, no knowing of home's blessedness. No sowing, no reaping. No perils, no discoveries.

Feb. 15. We held in our hand a check for $20,000.00! A mighty pretty sight for two penniless spectators. $3500.00 had been deducted for a new septic system and pump. Decision time had arrived. A fork in the road. Would we take the road less traveled? It's not how one feels, but how he deals. Our first defunct business venture had already been written off by the bank, but God does not defunct on His faithfulness. Our credit was in shambles, but we both knew that we had borrowed $17,000.00 with full intention of repaying every penny. The measure in which we take responsibility for our decisions is the measure in which our blessings flow - or not. Our house had not been repossessed.

We did not lose the escrow money, but graciously it was given back as a reward... **and a test.** We added up all we owed to creditors. Would it surprise you to know that everyone was paid the amount owed?

Shamefully I admit we had been on food stamps for the last three months, but the next time the mailman tooted his horn in my driveway for me to sign for the check, I turned him down. We were debt-free! We owed nothing to no-body....except our very lives to the Designer of it all. "Though the fig tree should not blossom, and there be no fruit on the vines, though... the fields produce no food, though the flock should be cut off from the fold, and there be no cattle in the stalls, yet I will exult in the Lord. I will rejoice in the God of my salvation!" Habakkuk 3:17-18, NASB.

I can laugh now at the one prerequisite the house inspector required before the deed was transferred to the new owners. The concrete piers under the old house must be reinforced with added concrete. The two of us mixed concrete ourselves and precariously slithered through a small opening on our bellies. The dirt on which I laid hadn't seen daylight in 100 years. Who knows what creatures would panic and demand our demise? What about that rat that had consumed all of our duck food? Me....with the weight of a whole house above my body! But Jesus had the weight of the world's sin laid right on Him. Lord, if I must smear concrete on ancient piers, so be it. Claustrophobic in daylight but, in the mysterious blackness, my mantra became, "You light my lamp, Lord; illumine my darkness! For only by You can I run upon a troop. By my God I can leap over a wall" Psalm 18:28-29, NASB ....or paste concrete with bare hands on a crumbling foundation! To die is gain! His death was the gain for anyone whose foundation is crumbling.

Alas! We were liberated to dwell in the Promised Land....for a season. "Call on Me in the day of trouble, and I will rescue you, and you will honor Me. He who offers a sacrifice of thanksgiving honors Me; and to him who orders his way aright I shall show the salvation of God." Psalm 50:15,23, NASB. All the miserable moments on Monte Vista Road did not hold a candle to all the blissful glee that God gifted us with in the western North Carolina mountains. If you see a piece of my heart still lying somewhere on the side of the road, treat it with care! No amount of coercion or correction can make it change its mind.

March 17. Safely tucked in on Vista Drive. The blizzard of the century quarantined the entire area. By the next afternoon twenty-five inches of pristine whiteness had buried every crocus, every promise that spring was in her dressing room. We all giggled and laughed over Chelsea's disappearance in the billowing clouds of cleanness, only to briefly glance at her body leaping like a whale soaring upward out of a placid glistening ocean; her graceful body would rise in pride and descend as quickly and gracefully, the snow engulfing her again into its depths. It was as if the heavens had released a pure, holy, and unctuous message: "Be still and know that I am God!" Psalm 46:10, NKJV. To Job (38:4-5, NASB): "Where were you when I laid the foundation of the earth? Tell Me if you have understanding. Who set its measurements? (v 6b-7) Who laid its cornerstone, when the morning stars sang together, and the sons of God shouted for joy? (v 28-29) Has the rain a father? Who begot the drops of dew? From whose womb has come the ice? And the frost of heaven, who has given it birth? (41:11) Who has given to Me that I should repay him? Whatever is under the whole heaven is Mine!"

Even at midnight, while soothing a fussy fifteen month old, the earth shone in unspoiled, uncorrupted newness. How often we sleep through such magical moments! "The moon on the breast of the new fallen snow gave the luster of midday to objects below."[16] I still keep near to me the picture of my fifteen month old Will, clad in a hand-me-down tattered yellow terry-cloth little bathrobe, as he awoke and spied a ten foot Christmas tree aglow with lights early one December morning. His mouth agape in wonderment is forever indelibly etched in my mind, and my prayer remains, "Oh, Lord, please, please, may I daily greet *You* with such amazement and as awestruck as this little child has these lights."

Icy excuses of busyness often kept me from feeling the warmth of His feathers; he lives to cradle me in coziness and quietness, but how I have shoved Him away, like a sleepy cranky two year old who will not slow down for fear he will crash. How often I still manage to keep my emotions hidden, striving for others to guess that my puzzle has fit together nicely and has been shelved. Perfectionists...people who go to great pains to give everyone else one! Would He ever throw up His hands in desperation and give up on me?

When would I realize that there really is power in weakness? What if what He really wants for me is hiding under all the shellac I've painted on, trying to cover my faults and fears? Gunk builds up. A disappointment here, a failure there. A bump in the road here, a wrong road chosen over there. It all begins to mask the true beauty that Jesus created us for. What if who He formed me to be is masked under layer upon layer of sticky unyielding resin because I refused to take the time and care necessary to strip it down to the original charm? Stripping furniture is a very arduous task when coat after coat of paint has been slathered on top of the old. What if, like that newly fallen snow, I would allow Jesus to scrape away the crimson colors of insecurity, pride, and phoniness, and let my imperfections shine as brilliantly as the moon on the whiteness? We are all "fearfully and wonderfully made." Psalm 139:14a, NASB. Jesus sees only beauty in what He "skillfully wrought in the depths of the earth" (v 15b), and, like a potter hovered over his lump of clay, Jesus formed each of us separately, individually, uniquely. Each infant who has ever sucked the air into his lungs has exceptional and matchless gifts, talents, and traits. Why do we labor to mask those mysterious marvelous gifts?

When the furniture's wood is finally exposed, the scratches, dents, and gouges only serve as beauty marks. The hardness of life's enigmas, the circumstances that crush, and the imperfections of interactions all add character to our beauty... the internal beauty He gaped over on our birth-day.

"Purify me with hyssop, and I shall be clean; wash me, and I shall be whiter than snow. Make me to hear joy and gladness, let the bones You have broken rejoice." Psalm 51:7-8, NASB. Hyssop was used to relieve pain; the herb branches were dipped in the blood of a sacrificial unblemished lamb and applied to the doorpost of the Jewish homes during the Egyptian captivity. Because the angel of death witnessed the covering of blood, the Israelite babies were "passed over" on his way to smite the Egyptian babies. God has, to fleshly eyes, strange ways to birth blessings.

Long long before Jesus actually appeared on earth, He sent numerous previews of the coming attraction...through prophecies, types, fore-shadowing. No blood, no life. No sacrifice, no access. No vulnerability, no intimacy. "No" to performance, but "Yes" to acceptance.

February 28. Sunday. I awoke several times during the night in an empty bed. Jack always rises early, so I guess I never checked the clock in the darkness. At 6:00 a.m. I awoke to an excited, beckoning call. My sweet man grabbed my hand and lifted me to my feet to the news that God had called him into full-time ministry. "It was so clear, Jill, we no longer have any debt, no "things" tying us down, nothing hinders us from serving! He could not use us when we owed so much to so many, but we are free now to cut loose and head down that road less traveled."

Joining the pastor in early morning Sunday prayer, Jack relayed his sudden new-found revelation. "What took you so long?" was the pastor's reply. "I've known this for months."

Inquiries were made from diverse seminaries. God had gifted Jack in managing, accounting, and discerning how to focus a big picture direction when presented with differing angles. Knowing he was not initially called to preach, he zeroed in on administration and religious education. Southwestern in Fort Worth, Texas, was hailed as the choice. We began our 1000 mile search for a home, knowing that I would need to return to teaching. With only one vehicle, living in student housing was a requisite. Many applications were snail-mailed back and forth before the age of instant notifications. Going without knowing. I felt like Abraham. Leave your city, your relatives, and your friends. Where am I going? I will show you. How long will it take? I will provide. I will bless you.

April 1. Because of my divorce, more paperwork. I was asked to elaborate, to give in detail, additional information before he would be accepted. How do I feel about being the spouse of one committed to vocational ministry? Describe your conversion, commitments, formative influences. Describe and evaluate your spiritual experiences. Press the pause button. Rewind the last five years of your life. Still I whined, "God, I do not have a story. Would you please write His-story on my life? I want a testimony!" If I had been Him, I would have been so so sarcastic in my reply..."Duh".

Prayers answered! It's easy to ask, but make sure you will eat anything laid on the table! There is no dessert unless you eat what's good for you! My last statement in my first written testimony read, "If Jack had not been sure that he had been chosen for such a time as this (marrying me and three children), I think it would have been extremely hard for him to have endured the ride. But...he has NO doubts! He has been God's vessel to give me new life; it would grieve my soul if my life in any way hindered his call."

Receiving word of our new address and an enclosed floor plan, we began to prepare for departure for fall semester. Assurance without seeing. FAITH. Too much "stuff" for a small two bedroom apartment. Knowing that we were to pitch our tent in Texas for two years, but not knowing where we would eventually settle, we divided belongings into "Take" and "Leave". A dear friend in Tennessee would store some belongings. A moving van would need to be rented so that we could DIY.

July 1. Van rented. Payment due on Monday. Sunday. The sweet people who had loved and cared for us for four years took up a love offering. The van had been rented with no visible means of support to pay for it! For the first time in a great while, I felt truly alive, for as the people lined up to greet us after church, it hurt to know parting. Mary Magdalene's grief over Jesus' death tears my heart anew every time it's read. Her loss led her back to the tomb, and she was inconsolably weeping. Her wound was laid open, raw, desperately in need of a healing balm. The angels asked her why she was crying. Through sobs and untethered gasps, she panted, "They have taken my Lord, and I do not know where they have laid Him." John 20:13, NASB. She turned, and spied someone behind her. Through crocodile tears she blurted out, "Sir, if you have carried Him away, tell me where you have laid Him, and I will carry Him away!" (v.15) Jesus tenderly replied, "Mary!"

Spilled out! Have you ever witnessed a good-bye scene at the airport or an army wife bid her soldier husband off to war? I made a vow that night that I would never open up myself to love so freely and completely again. The next two years I would live unaffected by love; it breaks your heart. Little did I know then that when one doesn't give it away, it hardens your heart.

One testimony to Southwestern, down. Another one to go, to our dear Asheville friends.

"Helen Keller once said, 'The best and most beautiful things in the world cannot be seen or even touched. They must be felt with the heart.' Our hearts indeed have truly been blessed by these four years of warm genuine fellowship with dear friends.

We are convinced that, on our journey of faith, we were sent here, not for Jack's job, but for the growth and refinement that only your contagious love for the Lord could offer. Please know that Jack and I take very seriously your shared sacrifices, not only today, but over the last difficult months. As today's difficulty is tomorrow's testimony, we pray we will wisely use and share your generosity, so that your precious gifts will be used to lay up treasures in heaven. All of your smiles and surprises have enriched our lives immeasurably. We have seen Jesus through your unselfishness, comfort, counsel, and love. The tears we cry upon our departure are filled with joy and sorrow: sorrow because you have endeared yourselves so tenderly to us, but joy because God is only washing our eyes so that we may know afresh of His providence and commandments."

The moving van was paid for, backed into our Vista Drive home; several men came to help load, and we had enough money left to get to Texas and pay the first month's rent. Jack loaded Blair and Walker in the cool moving van; Taylor, 3, Chelsea-dog, and I brought up the rear in our un-air-conditioned van, breathing in the last refreshment of mountain air and dropping off a piece of my heart. Why is it that in the midst of our most painful memories we find our most treasured ones?

7

Humpty Dumpty Had a Great Fall

Halfway point between North Carolina and Texas: West Tennessee. Roots. We stopped to leave half of our belongings but, most importantly, to hug my older boys' necks and greet our newest baby granddaughter! Alyssa became a big sister on her thirteenth month birth-date. Their family had graciously offered to care for Chelsea-dog for the two years that we would be away. Because they lived on a country road, I truly never expected to see her again. If I did not *know* that the Lord had asked me to write this I would quit right now, for every time a parting scene is revisited, my heart tears open again. Would my big boys ever know how many tears I have spilled and how I wished I'd never had to ask them to grow up before it was time? Call. Sing. Seek. Remember. "Do not touch My anointed ones," He proclaimed once upon a time...and still does. Psalm 105:15, NASB.

Over the Mississippi River and across flat Arkansas we traveled, on our way to a home we had never seen, one that was chosen for us by strangers. But home, like church, is not physical but a heart-plot where we are with those we love and who love us...warts and all. In hot mid-July, Taylor and I traipsed down Interstate-40, fetching every scrap of breeze that the yellow van dispatched. We were singing a song, when I glanced to the right and saw our yellow leader exiting as we sped on ahead. Little

Rock would be viewed on the periphery by part of us, while we would head straight through. No problem. No cell phones. No worry. No way to communicate. We would just pull over on the other side of town and wait for them to catch up. Over an hour sitting in the fumes of other cars scurrying on their way left us both drained and me a bit concerned. I spotted a near-by highway patrol station, pulled in, and asked for their assistance. Assured that they would find them, I began to slowly head west. Policemen always help us.

Another dilemma. Hungry and low on gas, I realized that all our money was with the man in the yellow van. Coming into Hope, Arkansas, we spotted a patrol car and explained our situation. He was clueless, had not been contacted to look out for Jack. "I will stop at a bank in Hope, write a check, and get some gas money, so please be on the look-out." Pulling in a parking space, it washed over me that we no longer had a checking account. Our account was closed out right before the move because that bank did not exist in Texas. I went in to beg for mercy. While attempting to make this complicated story a bit easier, I got a phone call...in a foreign place, an alien among strangers. Who knows me in Hope? But we are in Hope, the city of optimism, confident of deliverance! It was the highway patrol, stating that he had located the yellow van at the next exit. I actually turned down the money I was being offered, ecstatic and thankful to get out of this scrape. Our car was loaded with fine china and "stuff" we couldn't leave, but, when one is hungry and very hot, what we thought would bring us pleasure provides not even a dry crumb or one tiny whiff of fresh air. I skipped to the car headed for a needed reunion!

No yellow van in sight at the next exit! "God, isn't this what You asked us to do? We are obeying. Dare I ask if this is what the next two years will hold?" Mt. Pleasant, Texas, is a l-o-n-g way from Memphis, Tennessee, and I was cruising on fumes. No money. Emotions hanging on by a thin thread. How difficult it was to look at a hungry three year old with beads of sweat pouring down his face and neck! How could You look on Your *thirty*-three year old with blood drops beading up all over the parched earth? He was thirsty, too.

Was It You, Lord, who caused me to eye a streak of yellow to my left perched on the last hill? We pulled off the side of the interstate, praying that the van in our rear view mirror held our loved ones. We waited for an eternity. That van must be there waiting to be rented; it's been there too long. No, wait! It's moving, pulling out toward the exit. P-le-e-a-s-s-s-e let it be them! It slowed then stopped behind us. Never have I been so overjoyed to be in the arms of loved ones! We all kissed and danced and hugged right on the side of the road. How could I get so far on one tank of gas? Mt. Pleasant was mighty pleasant that day, but God provided the banquet. "Open your mouth wide and I will fill it!" Psalm 81:10, NASB. Boy, oh boy, did we want it! Rain on us! "I will feed you with the finest of wheat; and with honey from the rock I will satisfy you!" (v 16). Such valuable food provided from the unlikeliest of places. Bring Yourself on! The enemy will not destroy what You have prepared for those who love You. Satan's Welcome-to-Texas mat was jerked out from under him. His desire for Little Rock to be our Big Stumbling Boulder led to Hope and ultimately to salvation in the Mount of Pleasantries. Hallelujah!!

8

The Mouse Ran Up the Clock

Following seminary directions, our caravan wend its way to a most welcome sight. My sister Katie, a Louisiana resident, had agreed to meet us in Fort Worth to help out. With no way to communicate our delay, she had waited over four hours for our arrival. The children were whisked off the next morning to the zoo.

Two bedrooms. Three children...an almost 13 year old girl and two little brothers, 4 and 16 months. One week-maybe-unworkable! We decided to donate the bedrooms to the kids and sleep on the let-out bed in the living room.

To find a teaching position which would begin in less than a month proved to be perplexing and frustrating. This was in the early 90's, so applying via computer was not the norm yet. I was not the "early bird who would catch the worm". However, in a district just south of Fort Worth, I did have an interview the week school started; blossoming beyond expectation in numbers, the system needed an extra teacher. On Friday afternoon, with school set to commence on Monday, I was offered a third grade position. Scurrying to find daycare and then needing to heed the directions to convert an old empty science lab into an inviting classroom over the weekend, I initiated the impossible. Also encumbered with new teaching manuals and with a "whole language" system of instruction, I was as fresh tar on a roadbed flattened by an oncoming steamroller. Added to this assignment, I must care for three children and a newly enrolled husband in seminary, who had picked up a side job in the carpentry shop at the school. He would be responsible for taking care of student housing issues that needed repaired.

No sleep for three days. Like a fall pumpkin scraped and hollowed out for its carved happy face, I painted on a smile for a new group of eight year olds, marched into the principal's office during PE, and resigned the same day I began. How could I offer a gift I did not possess? So very much to do, so little time. How would I ever arrive at daycare by 5:00 p.m. or be ready and glowing in the a.m. for twenty-something eager-faced active third graders? I was sucked in a vortex of hopelessness. My fellow teachers had also made it very clear that this district was tops and that parents were demanding and tough. Confidence and optimism vanished. Disintegrated.

"A joyful heart is good medicine, but a broken spirit dries up the bones." Proverbs 17:22, NASB. "Hope deferred makes the heart sick." Proverbs 13:12, NKV. At the time there seemed to be no trace of a pathway back to the land of the living. Job confessed, "He has fenced up my way, so that I cannot pass, and He has set darkness in my paths" (19:8, NKJ) Truthfully, this DIY girl was once again being led by an "I have to do this, and I have to do it well, right now" mentality. So many hot shards of sand whipped in my face in this desert that I had no time to even consider the One who could water my soul. My anticipations of what I expected from myself far over-shadowed what my superiors and my husband deemed necessary. I was part of the wordly cultural caste system. Its love affair with "self-help" wisdom travels on diverse tracks with the wisdom of resting in Jesus.

Right or wrong. Good or bad. God's will or my self-preservation. I know not, only that He is faithful, and, even in my infidelity, He remained loyal. My husband needed me, and I had quit....given up treading water to sink our family. That first week of school, Blair mentioned over supper that she could tell us how to be initiated into a gang. The rough neighborhood surrounding Southwestern was instructing her in ungodliness. At least now I was home to search for alternative schooling for her. Fort Worth had several magnet schools, and she was accepted in a program only several miles from home.

Drafting a letter to each principal in the Fort Worth Independent School System, I asked about any possible last minute openings. Our love money from Asheville was dangerously low. Running on fumes was about to be our constant way of life. Mid-September brought a call concerning an opening on the far eastern side of town, which I accepted. Whether consequences from previous independence or just God's call to bloom there in adversity, I know not. But for the next eight months, I was a fish floundering out of water. Communication with leadership seemed to be as dead as a smoke alarm without batteries. Moses was slow of speech and greatly surprised when God called him to deliver the Israelites from slavery, but God gave him perfect counsel and faultless promises: A B C...1 2 3. Jonah said no to a task, but he had been told exactly where to go and what to do. March around Jericho quietly for six days seemed a preposterous request, but they knew what was expected of them. Gideon was reared in poverty and was the youngest, but God sent him to deliver the Jews from Midian, instructing him in detail which three hundred soldiers to call to arms. Being a compassionate, skilled, and involved mentor is absolutely crucial to the development of your underlings. But I was employed and thankful for His provision.

We could not afford to travel "home" for Christmas, and Jack had work which he would be allowed to do over the break. Campus emptied out like a purse's contents dumped for cleaning. Cars departed in all directions, homeward bound and laden with cheer. Jack announced his invitation to host a family of six from

Maryland for Christmas dinner. "What do you want me to feed them?" I retorted, "We are having pinto beans and cornbread!" God will provide, ye one of little faith

Did I not remember Asheville's deliverance from bank bondage and foreclosure to freedom? A benevolent church's love gift? A beautiful yellow van in Mt. Pleasant, Texas? A job in Fort Worth? Why are we so stubborn and stiff-necked? Need I wander 40 years to learn Thy lesson? "He saved them (His own) for His name's sake, that He might make His power known." Psalm 106:8, NKJ. Please, Lord, do it again! "Satisfy my thirsty soul and fill my hungry soul with what is good!" Psalm 107:9, NASB. Spying a small plastic tree at the local "dime" store, I visited daily the week before Christmas to see if a "Sale" tag had been attached. Yeah! December 23 (the day the house in North Carolina sold), with tree in hand, I danced home to unveil my surprise. Jack welcomed me and handed over a card: "May your Holy-days be filled with the love of our Savior!" And out fell $50.00 from our pastor's family in Asheville! Oh, W-O-W!

"The spiritual life is the life of a child. We are not uncertain of God, just uncertain of what He is going to do next. As soon as we abandon to God, and do the task He has placed closest to us, He begins to fill our lives with surprises."[17] Oswald Chambers' little snippet sent all I needed for Christmas.

His cleansing and scrubbing of my unbelief washed my dirty fickleness. Living like many baby Christians, I confessed my belief in Jesus, without claiming access to His power: "dunamos" or dynamite! Simple celebrations and importunate prayers create mighty miracles out of wee blessings. "Oh, happy day when Jesus washed my sins away! He taught me how to watch and pray, and live rejoicing every day!"[18]

Our first summer led to more surgeries for Walker's back. The once dermabraded "war zone" had not been successfully routed, so the unsightly blackness had reappeared. Isn't that sin at its root? One can't leave a trace of dandelion underpinning if another "lion's tooth" is not welcome to sprout. Even a little leaven causes bread to rise. One small worm rots an entire apple.

The surgeon excised an inch above and an inch below the incision, planning on whittling down the massive nevus, and he stitched him up 'til the next time. Our daughter-in-law and two granddaughters visited us; news was imparted that she and John were divorcing. Our second son Will came, too, and spent that week grieving the break-up with his girlfriend. Guilt raised its ugly head to taunt this mother for going AWOL.

My job had been a one year position, so the search was on again. I received an offer much closer to home and for tutoring at-risk children. Our two years in Texas was at the half-way point. My vow in leaving Asheville to get close to no one was faithfully pocketed and kept close. Having little time for relationships was one thing, but closing oneself off to others' encouragement and nurturing was starving my soul. Biding my time, crossing off calendar days, and suffocating myself with future fantasies of settling down in Canaanland, I kept myself moving mindlessly through this self-inflicted wandering. Even church, where we mingled and pretended to savor its delicacies, was only a temporary tabernacle. Around many or few, no one knew of the loneliness. No one knew that I hated hot weather and lack of seasons, that I still yearned for the security of my baby blanket, that ...even a church co-worker called Jack "Stan". All three guys had first and last names that could be interchanged.

All I desired was to be the savior for Will in his grief and to bandage the gaping wound for single-again John. But almost a year passed before we two even conversed. Considering that I had supported his ex-wife's "side", he felt critically wounded by my judging his actions. And Texas was too far from Tennessee to dig fence posts. C. S. Lewis stated somewhere, "Friendship is unnecessary, like philosophy, like art...it has no survival value; rather it is one of those things that gives value to survival."

The Sunday School scene in Tennessee the weeks after our marriage began an avalanche of His writing His message to me on a canvas banner across the sky. "For the believer all pain has meaning; all adversity is profitable. It usually takes us by surprise and appears completely senseless and irrational. But God has a purpose in every pain He brings or allows in our lives, either for our profit or His glory."[19]

"I am building for you the testimony you prayed for. 'My thoughts are not your thoughts, neither are your ways My ways. For as the heavens are higher than the earth, so are My ways higher than your ways, and My thoughts than your thoughts. For as the rain and snow come down from heaven, and do not return without watering the earth, and making it bear and sprout.... so shall My Word be which goes forth from My mouth; it shall not return to Me empty, without accomplishing what I desire and without succeeding in the matter in which I sent it'." Isaiah 55:8-10, NASB.

Was it really just my fancy that He would zap me into a cypress from a thorn bush? His invitation to the hungry is to come, buy, and eat without money or cost. If I would listen and accept His offer, I could delight myself in abundance. The wealth of Washington D.C. could never afford His nourishment. The food has already been bought and paid for. Just take it from His open hand.

Graduation Day loomed ahead like a desert mirage, fueling hope that we would soon "arrive". But Jericho didn't fall without obedience to His calling. Randy Pausch in *The Last Lecture* stated, "Brick walls are there for a reason. They give us a chance to show how badly we want something. Once you get over them, even if someone has practically had to throw you over them, it can be helpful to others to tell them how you did it."[20] His philosophy of enduring failure only as a learning tool for success left his children an astute legacy, but spiritual matters trump intellectual ones every single time. S-u-c-c-e-s-s is spelled J-e-s-u-s.

Like baby spiders scatter from a squashed egg sack, "our" resumes reached their tentacles in varied directions. Seminary housing had to be vacated by July 31, so boxes began to be stuffed with possessions and psalms of praise for our entrance into Beulahland ("My delight is in her.").[21] Nothing but the ticking of the clock. Lord, did You lead us here, only to leave us stuck in the heat of the Texas wind?

July 11. Graduation....just the five of us. Sitting in the worship center surrounded by celebrating families vacuumed up every particle of confetti I was set to throw. Feast Day had arrived, but I was overcome with loneliness, coveting that family could have joined us in the killing of the fatted calf. But surely Abba must feel the same way: He created us so that we could fellowship with Him. How many times do I see His hand in beauty... in sunsets, flowers, breezes, the adorable goats pasturing down the road, a child's tiny handclasp, and in other people's kindnesses and smiles...but fail to acknowledge and thank Him? How often do I just stand still and smile at Him? How my busyness must tally up teeming times that He has been lonely for me to hallow His holiness or rest in His embrace? O, Lord, disintegrate me.

July 18. A job offer in Fort Worth. Lord, surely You jest in this testing, for the church people do not hold to many of our beliefs.

July 24. A call from Mississippi. "Our pastor and search chairman would like to fly to Dallas to interview you...both of you."

July 25. A call from Tennessee, only three hours from the boys! "Could you please fly up next week?" Next week? But that's eviction week!

Like Habakkuk we were e-v-e-r s-l-o-w-l-y learning to station ourselves on the watchtower to see what He would speak to us. "For the vision is yet for the appointed time; it hastens toward the goal, and it will not fail. Though it tarries, wait for it;

for it will certainly come, it will not delay." Habakkuk 2:3, NASB. I was a child waiting for Christmas morning, but it always took much too long to arrive.

Unlike Elijah, set firmly in his concrete faith as he poured gallons of water on the slain oxen and altar, I still dwelt in the mire of quicksand, *hoping* He would show, not ASSURED the He would. Not..."Today let it be known that You are the God of Israel, and that I am Your servant, and that I have done all these things at Your Word. Answer me, Lord, answer me, that this people may KNOW that Thou, O Lord, art God, and Thou has turned their heart back again." I Kings 18:36-37, NASB. But, more like..."Oh, Lord, if You decide that You would like us to move..... Are You *really paying attention* to this little problem of ours?" I proclaimed that I was a Christ-follower but still denied His power and compassion, that He truly was right in our midst, closer than my own breathing.

Because Jack worked in seminary maintenance, he was asked to stay an extra week to prepare student housing for the fall semester; our new deadline was now August 6!

July 29. Airport interview with two gentlemen from Mississippi.

July 30. On a plane for Tennessee interview. In a hotel room while there, we received a call from the Mississippi pastor. "What are you doing there?"

"How did you find us?"

"Never mind that...You will not be a Volunteer!"

August 2. On a plane for Mississippi's second interview.

From no job in sight to two choices! How do we know your will, Lord? We are ready and willing, but, please, Lord, let it be Tennessee! Renting would need to be our required housing because of our lack of funds for a down payment. Like air escaping from a birthday balloon, the housing situation in Tennessee orbited in circular paths downward and shriveled into flatness. But in Mississippi a church member just "happened" to overhear a Wednesday night meal conversation and offered us a rental three bedroom house which had just been vacated! No.... he determined to sell us the house and finance the sale himself. Our own yard. Our own neighborhood. Our own blank canvas on which we could color our world with the pastels of His love! Carry us home, Sweet Chariot!

9

How Does Your Garden Grow?

August 6. Home. The clock had struck 11:59 p.m. God *had* come through, not a minute too early, but not a minute late. Do on do, rule on rule, a little here, a little there. Blocks tumble when the foundation is shaky. Learn your lessons thoroughly. Crawl before you walk. Drink from the sippy cup before the goblet. Scars are only formed after a wound is inflicted. "Truly, truly, I say to you. Unless a seed falls into the ground, and it dies, it remains by itself alone; but if it dies, it bears much fruit." John 12:24, NASB. To gaze at a seed, one can hardly comprehend that, deep inside its hardness, a beauty-full life has already been determined, implanted, and embraced. Its being buried and broken is actually its renewal...its revival. "The development of the divine life in the Christian is like the natural growth in the vegetable world. We do not need to make any special effort, only place ourselves under the conditions for such growth. Only those who have sought to grow by effort and have failed are in the position to appreciate the fact that God is the aggressor in the realm of development."[22]

After Jesus died and was raised there were skeptics about His resurrection and how God could and would raise His children. In I Corinthians 15 Paul addressed what looks like an impossibility. "What you sow does not come to life unless it dies. And as for what you sow-you are not sowing the future body, but only a seed, perhaps of wheat or another grain. But God gives it a body as He wants, and to each seed its own body. (v 36-38, HCSB) Resurrection and life with Christ *will* be a reality for those who believe that He is who He says He is and confess that without shame. He gave us a heads-up in Romans as He relays, "For since the creation of the world My invisible attributes, My power, My divine nature have been clearly seen and understood through what I have made, so men are without excuse." Romans 1:20, NASB. He shows us every single spring; resurrection occurs as we turn the soil over, lay a tiny hard kernel into barrenness, and bury what appears to be ugly. But don't we faithfully expect something beautiful to arise? The newborn sprout first pops its head up to awaken the morning, and we rejoice! But, with water and warmth of light, glory emerges bit by bit! That which is sown does not come to life until it dies; it falls apart. There is indeed a difference between what is laid down and what arises.

Like a good teacher, God models to us by what we can see, so that we will believe that what we cannot see is absolutely as real! Hallelujah! John MacArthur says of the Christian that we are "holy seeds encased in unholy shells. Incarcerated in a prison of flesh and subjected to its weaknesses and imperfections, we eagerly await an event that is guaranteed but is yet to transpire-the redemption of our bodies."[23] If Christ has been invited to invade my heart, the "stuff" encased inside the seed pod of my bodily tent disintegrates, and He morphs it into a new beautiful creation, albeit one that won't burst forth until He calls me home to glory. But it's morphing is sure because He says it is. J. Vernon McGee said it aptly, "The old creature has no good; the new creation has no power."

Even though I am still encased in the flesh after re-creation, I am still none-the-less beauty-full to Him....and to the world, too, if I simply rest in the cold hardness of the world and allow Him to pull out the glory when and how He sees fit. And one day, like the nursery fairy in *The Velveteen Rabbit,* who burst forth from Rabbit's tears to gather him up into her arms and kiss his wet nose, Abba will do the same for each of His own. Simplistic, yes, but a shadowy illustration of what it will truly be like when my old dingy hind legs (or whatever fortresses I have hidden behind on earth) suddenly dance on heavenly turf! Twisting upward in pirouettes, whirling around His throne, and bowing in adoration will assuredly grant the knowledge that, at last, I am finally HOME.

Can I snugly sit in my pew Sunday after Sunday encased in smugness? Are my hands so clean that I can't mess with trailer trash? Dare I judge my granddaughter's decision to move in with her boyfriend after having known the sting of her mommy/daddy divorce? How can I not bear-hug the child at the neighborhood school whose mama never gathers her chicks around a dinner table or reads a bedtime story? How about the women imprisoned in their own homes, living with men who know not how to be a tender husband? Or the innumerable single mothers weary and worn, striving to fulfill dual roles? These lives are encased in poverty of spirit; they have little chance to be watered or to feel the warmth of the Sonlight. How often we sterile redeemed stay enclosed in the hardness of our shells, unwilling to die, to be crucified, to make allowance for any vulnerability that just might crack our self-imposed prison doors open?

Dan Allender rightly relayed, "Suffering is necessary for us because it strips away the pretense that life is reasonable and good, a pretense that keeps us looking in all the wrong places for the satisfaction of our souls."[24] We *thought* we were finally HOME, we *felt* like we were HOME, but it was just a shell in which we would abide safely for a season. And while inside that Mississippi manger cave on Windsor Drive, our Father would shepherd us, as He gently but deliberately led us through several dry weary Texas summers."The Lord is my shepherd; there is nothing I lack." Psalm 23:1, HCSB. His path, though less-traveled, has nevertheless been worn down by all those who have chosen to go before, as He restores, guides, strengthens, feeds, clothes, and offers His little ones sweet green pastures.

Little did we know on moving day which parade floats we would ride on next. Are we ever given test answers before a test? Would we ride a red, white, and blue bannered bicycle in the heat of July? Would it be a Fat Tuesday celebration of myriad colors of confetti, as we partied before the fasting? Would it be in our Easter bonnets, strutting spring pastels? Or wrapped in the gray warmth of earmuffs and boots in the Christmas parade?

In the movie "Out of Africa" Robert Redford was told by Meryl Streep, "God made the earth round so that we couldn't see what lay ahead of us on down the road." Lesson upon lesson, grade on grade, a little here a little there. Why do we often think we have arrived when we truly haven't even pulled out of the station?

10

London Bridge is Falling Down

Parallel tracks...

Jack carried me across a sliding glass door that refused to lock, so a broom handle would be our security system. Our "new" home vs squatter termites. Home cookin' vs lingering Far Eastern kitchen cuisine odors. Closet space vs holes in sheetrock. Windows to view His world vs grime, bugs, and ivy. Hardwood floors vs nasty green shag carpeting. Laundry room vs leaky roof. A real bargain vs cost of overwhelming DIY projects. Dad's new job vs Mom's three children, one entering grade 9, another grade 1, and a three year old.

Bless this house, O Lord, I pray. Bless me, Jehovah, as I seek to build my nest in this Land of Opportunity. Closets could not be filled until cleaned and painted. Isn't that life? The parts of us that aren't visible to others have clutter and filth that desperately need Clorox and knee-bent weeding; how tempting it was to shove our "stuff", our seeds which would be unseen, in on top of dirt, just so that the blossoms, which are visible, could burst forth. Forcing maturity is not God's way. The ivy clinging to the bedroom window prevented morning Sonlight from sating us, but, when pulled away, it left sticky little tentacles of goo. There was no easy fix for the ivy removal or the closet renovation. Paint won't stick to grime. Rough shelving would do

77

no more for any of us than splinter our fingers and cause pus to fester. Sometimes surgery is all that will heal the wound. Heal the wound of exhaustion but leave the scar of renewal, for clean closets will remind us of Your faithfulness. Open my eyes to see glimpses of truth You have for me in the pretenses of my DIY attitudes. You, Jehovah, prepare me by setting up struggles in which my closet life vies with my living room life. Pretending to be self-less but wholly self-living. You know what I need, Lord, but I'm too scared to ask. Just do it!

Working the fingers from dawn until midnight is not His desire, but living out of cardboard boxes was not my idea of living. If only I had repented and rested, keepin' the main thing the main thing. If only I had found rest in quietness and trusting. If God works slowly but patiently, then why do I find it necessary to create order from chaos in a few quick days?

My dealing with a child pulling on my leg craving attention, as well as my desire for fellowship with a new friend, lathered our home atmosphere with whining. Exhausted by long hours at a new job, my husband limped in nightly needing nourishment for his tummy and his spirit. But I was more worried about what he would "think" was left undone. Tears became my food. I remember hanging over the stove, striving to make breakfast but unable to move. I had felt crummy for weeks but attributed it to exhaustion.

Sitting in the doctor's office, I was handed a questionnaire and left alone, legs dangling off the examining table. The doctor was occupied elsewhere, so his not returning in my due time, I glanced at the paperwork on the desk and scored my own test. Severe depression. Down as low as the scale went. This kaleidoscope of darkness at least had a name, albeit being a black sheep in a new community was not what I coveted.

This DIY girl hung by a thread of falling into the abyss of total hopelessness. Like my near-by Qaneh, I was nothing but a shell.

A gusty wind could have done me in. Gaping holes negate a wall's insulation. Rusty implements clutter a yard.

Tarps are band-aids against rotten shingles. Rats have a shopping spree through vacant rooms. The bucket at the well would never draw water again. Grass can't grow on ground stomped hard by a stampede of unmet expectations. Exactly what had I expected? That after a hard season of time in Texas I deserved for life to be "normal" again? That my self-imposed two year exile from hospitable hearts of women there would bring immediate bosom buddies? That my anorexic attitude would quickly be sated with the richest of His foods? That I could build my nest of orderliness and beauty overnight? That my daughter would not be one bit disappointed that ninth grade was still "middle school" in Mississippi? That church staff would be one big happy cohesive family of unity and support...especially when the pastor was called to another place just three months after our arrival?

Unmet human expectations are monsters hiding in the closet. They eat away at one's soul, never making an appearance except in the blackness of night. Unleashing their toxic threats, they are only harmful to the worn and weary.

No room in the inn anywhere to be found to the one pregnant and troubled and far from home. Did Mary's tears fall, too? Did her veins pulse with thick syrup and her surroundings close in like a soupy morning fog? What on earth am I doing here?

I am right where God has sovereignly and supremely placed me. Isaiah 30:15 (HCSB) says, "You will be delivered (from daily pitfalls) by returning and resting; your strength will lie in quiet confidence (in Him)." (Parenthesis mine) You surely recognize the verse to which I cling! The testimony plea that I had prayed six years earlier was still being manufactured day by day, rule on rule. No place to go but HOME. HOME to the open arms. He was crouched down with wide-stretched arms to receive, even in....no, especially in...my weakness. To this child running was not an option; crawling was all I could muster.

The doctor placed me on an anti-depressant and instructed me to return in three weeks. Closets had been revamped and painted, so I rejoiced at the pile of cardboard at the street. But the kitchen was screaming for help. Isn't that just like the world? One fleshly victory promises us supreme happiness, but, after its appeasing, it quietly fades away, taunting its hollow choruses on its way out the door. The only refreshment to my soul was the hope that this pill's magic potion would soon scatter the demons in my path. Hunkering down low into a deep recessed kitchen cabinet, I began to dredge the debris of someone else's story in a house that now bore my name.

Febreeze, plug-ins, and candles.....all cover-ups...to keep the filth from stench.

Old receipts...."If I need to return it" or maybe to rationalize to the husband "what a great deal I got" or (I can hear her now) "But we needed it; you get paid tomorrow!"

Half used bottle of vinegar..."Why is this cleaning and restoring agent so rotten, so rank?" We so often do not like the way chosen for us to be scrubbed pure; whining is much easier.

Silly straw... Qaneh the "reed": "Just suck it up and try, try again"...or better yet... "Silly sounds like so much fun! Wish my feet would dance!"

Throw it all away! It's trash...garbage...refuse. Just like sin, we hoard things we should get rid of, little things that eat away at the very foundations, just small misunderstandings, masks, charades. Suddenly, right smack in the middle of misery, crouched down in a nasty kitchen nook, my mood lightened! "Go write this down," I heard in crevice of my mind's eye. I grabbed a near-by greeting card; on its cover I perused "One Wonderful You, 1000 Reasons to be Thankful!" Just when one needs it the most, God grants a memo, not a meltdown! Hallelujah! A whiff of joy earthquaked my pensiveness. "What you are doing is a type of what I am doing in and through you, a peeling away of particles of infected sores in you."

"Well, just do it...and hurry up!"

Four packets of sugar...sweetness in hiding.

Can opener...sharpness wasted.

Three brown sugars...hard from being unused.

Roll of ribbon...waiting to adorn a gift that was never received. "Lord, how many presents You have wrapped for us for the taking. Why do we so often ignore this Love?"

Torn circle form a pop-up memory book....visibility to see little smiling faces!

Garage sale stickers...5, 10, 50 cents... make an offer to cart our junk away.

A family picture.... We are all together again, we're here, we're here....but left forgotten.

An expired coupon... Enjoy life while you can. "Teach us to number our days, that we might present to You a heart of wisdom." Psalm 90:12, NASB.

Expired can of cake icing....sweetness turned sour...stay connected to the Vine.

Several stuck-together Kool -Aid packages.... Through thick or thin, we adhere.

Night light bulb...to light the way in the dark.

Razor blade...cuts through the gunky mire...or cuts you...all in the way it's handled.

Dicer... Pare down. Simplify.

A LOT of sticky residue...eroded the paint, all the way down to the raw wood. Spills not removed in due time become obstinate, merciless, callous, tough. Weeds always grow hardy, never a fragile stem. Wondering how one could live like this, the cocked finger not only pointed forward, but back right at me. Ouch.

    Two weeks. Three weeks. Clouds still reigned thick and dark. Fifty milligrams went to 100 mg. "Come back in three weeks."
    I should be better. I would if I could. I ought to...
    May flowers and spring days still could not cheer my soul. Now all three children would soon be home for three months. I *must* quit crying. I should be more patient. I ought to picnic, play, persevere. "Lord, I dread going to bed because I don't want to wake up to more of this mundaneness." Plopping down in a

dining room chair, my head bowed on the table, I came clean with Abba. If He counted my tears and agony that day, He surely filled a river. "Lord, I simply cannot DO this any longer!" Like the little blue engine, I chugged, "I cannot. I cannot. I cannot." Oh, that I knew where I might find God, that I might come to His seat! Job 23:3, NASB.

It was at that moment of complete surrender that (I know not whether aloud or in my spirit) I sensed six **beautiful deep Daddy words**, "Jill, this is for a purpose!"

Well, I did not feel better that day or for many more days to follow, but this DIY girl morphed into an HIS girl – His In Service. I was escorted from fear and failure to assurance of His pledge of care. Even though time ticked slowly that summer, I was not afraid of going crazy.

At 300 mg of that drug, I was drug into the Sonshine!! "I am not silenced by the darkness, nor the deep gloom that has covered me!" Job23:17, NASB.

"The Lord hears the needy and does not despise *His* who are prisoners." Psalm 69:33, NASB. "I tuned out to tune in", as Ann Ortland relays, "Only those who live well, die well!" Our testimonies are forged deep within dark places; He weaves our days together wonderfully, composes secretly His plan for each one of His children, and engraves each name on the palm of His hand. But we must allow Him to chip away at the hardness and the strongholds that hold us in prison. We DIY girls need rest from our labors. Retaking a course allows for reinforcing the lesson; even after the graduation ceremony, days come in which I think I can do it myself and can do it better.

Several articles of clothing worn during my dark days continued to be a red flag to my recovery. I remember going to a big church function in New Orleans wearing a dress I had loved: green and white small plaid with a tiny Nehru collar. Every time I subsequently wore that outfit, I remember a hazy, out-of-my-skin experience. Souvenirs are kept for times when our souls have been sated with joy. So, my freshly painted closet exported a box-full of its contents. New creatures wear royal robes, not the old striped uniforms of prison life!

Knowing I needed to get out for fresh air, I accepted a part-time position at the Christian school in which we had placed our boys. While in the workroom I overheard another assistant saying she could not understand her sadness and her desire to withdraw. "I have a wonderful husband, my kids are happy and healthy. What's goin' on?" During the next several months, our paths crossed several times, and the Lord gave me an open door. Like an overturned glass spreading its liquid across the table and through the cracks, my testimony spilled out all over her. My story seemed to sop up her dreariness and misunderstanding that Christian women should not be joy-sapped, nor ever consider chemical imbalances and family propensities to depression.

Another teacher, during a noisy cafeteria lunch one day, was lamenting about her retired husband's lack of activity. "All he does is sit in his chair. It drives me crazy that he is so listless and apathetic." Out of the mouth of a fellow prisoner came the truth, pregnant with impulse but delivered through experience, "Ann, *he* wants to get better much worse than you want him to!" Later, she thanked me profusely for changing her attitude and being more compassionate....not I dear one, not I, but the Giver of gifts.

Before the next year was over, I accepted a teaching position. One of my room mothers, who had previously been extremely active, began passing on her responsibilities and sending her two boys home with a friend. It wasn't long before God orchestrated another opportunity to seize the day.

And then there was the mother whose husband decided he thought another woman was more deserving of his affections...

Yes, He did have a purpose!

And in the years to follow.....more opportunities to walk in another's moccasins.

11

Diddle Dumpling, My Son John

The next spring we got a call from our son John that his dad had suffered a stroke. We packed up the car and headed north to a Memphis hospital. The calendar was dated March 21, the same date we two had once pledged our vows to each other. Forty-eight years young. He never regained consciousness. Three days later we escorted our oldest three to his funeral. Blair was 15.

"Lord, the best of our years are filled with pain and trouble. Soon they disappear, and we are gone. Who can comprehend Your power? Teach us to make the most of our time, so that we may grow in wisdom. Satisfy us in the morning with Your unfailing love. Let our children see Your glory at work. May You show us Your favor and confirm for me the work of my hands." My prayer from Psalm 90:10-17, selected verses.

Once frozen in fear and depression over a kitchen stove, unable to prepare a meal or a table for my family, failure had shamed and teased me. Standing in the exact same spot two weeks later, news arrived that caused me to gaze upward in adulation, not downward in despair. The wall calendar, displaying a jaunty joker that April 1 day, branded my heart with an ironic memorandum. Tears of thanksgiving flowed to the Preparer of blessings. The child support that I had forfeited in Asheville three years prior to this date was now deposited in my bank account three-fold, for Blair's dad's Social Security would be meted out for the next three years, until she turned 18.

I stand not in judgment or with my "Why?" questions, expecting an answer from the Provider. He is sovereign; He has the right to do whatever He wishes. All I know is that I will continue to love Him for better or worse, in plenty and want, because death will not part us.

Tenth grade greeted Blair with great gladness, and she linked in nicely with the "in" crowd. God designed us for relationships, and girls spend their entire seven teen years exhaustingly searching for their identity. She whirled into those years as Scarlett into Tara. As necessary as growing up is, growing away from mom and dad is like the mighty Mississippi after the spring rains, inundating its bluffs with churning forceful muddy energy and instigating a massive muddle of destruction. Girlfriends draw tight circles which inevitably leave someone out. Proverbs 12:26 warns us to be cautious in friendships, but, in an effort to fit in, girls quickly grab the straw of acceptance before prudence.

Girls need to be connected, to be intimate, to commiserate, even from pre-school days, but the spark of girl connections is fueled by flames of hormones into a blazing fiery inferno of uncontrolled emotions. "Hesed", the Hebrew word for unfailing love, combines the idea of mercy or kindness and faithfulness. *Friendships of Women* relays how women yearn for "hesed" from others and from the Lord. "We want our friends to be kind to us and to never abandon us. We want the kindness of friends intertwined with the permanence of family."²⁵

Sugar and spice and everything nice, pigtails, butterfly kisses, and smocked dresses erode into fittin' in, gettin' in, and stayin' in. Not hugs from Daddy anymore but affirmation from peers. They ask for your opinion only to turn in the opposite direction. "That check you receive from my daddy is mine to do with as I please."

"Which skirt do you like the best?" only so she can reverse Mama's decision. Asking for clarification on an outing, we are labeled as nosy.

And car keys? Drivers' license privileges? Soon after our 15 year old had her permit securely in hand, she headed me home from a mall excursion. Left blinker on, light turned green, and she headed down the divided highway straight into on-coming traffic! Ashamed to admit, but true, my very first reaction was to duck under the dash and pretend that this wasn't happening. "Drive into the median, Blair!" Isn't navigating life just as tense for youth as it is for parents?

"Bye, Mom, headed to Melanie's." Well, she *did* drive straight to Melanie's, put the car in park, turned the engine off, switched it back on, and contentedly drove to a banned destination. There was no lie involved in her taut rubber band of truth! Today's parents cannot fathom life without cell phones.

Sophomore English classes were given several novels to read. Her assigned book was abandoned on the dining room table, so I began to thumb through its pages, agape with disbelief over what fifteen year olds were being asked to consume. Like Tootle the train, watching butterflies and playing in a field of daisies when he should have been on the track, red flags began to pop up behind every bush in my mind. Our daughter was not going earn an A+ in maturity by reading this "literature". Immoral relationships, cursing, impure activities-all in the name of broadening a child's worldview? The teacher was called and asked if he would please approve an alternative selection, but, sadly, he considered us intolerant, judgmental, and narrow-minded.

Blair was informed that she was being enrolled in the private Christian school in which I taught. Hers would be the first class to graduate; eleven students would close out the 20th century. Many mile markers loomed ahead, none of which she was jealous to claim. In her estimation, we were tattooing her to a life of doom and gloom. Her skirts were required to be as long as her dangling fingertips. How could we be so cold? Jack's pre-date interview "scares away all prospective dates"!

But graduate she did, with her senior picture sporting a shoulder tattoo, as if to prove she did it her way. The freedom of college life with all its tinsel and glittery temptations lay right in front of her, like a greyhound madly racing around in circles, resolved to capture a dangling rabbit just out of reach, which was, from the race's outset, manipulated by a remote external sly mechanism. We might be on a tandem bicycle, thinking we are in control, but Jesus is the One in charge-totally and completely- of our journey's destination.

Rush week led to a sorority offer, which led to the fulfillment of a girl's dream to belong. But one finds out quickly that often what we think we want turns into a bad dream. No longer than it took to pay for the clothes she bought to "get in", she "got out".

"I am not going to let them dictate to me when and where and what I can and cannot do!" As surely as our "in-boxes" fill up with unordered solicitations, her soul was brimming full of spam. Her dad and I stood in the gap with prayer, holding up arms that resisted our touch. "Take the shackles off her feet so she can dance. We just want her to praise You. Break the chains; lift her hands."[26]

Blair thought her roommate unfriendly. Her teachers were unfair. Shenanigans closed too early. Church was stuffy. One semester down, already on academic probation!

"Finding ourselves in the fire of sorrow makes you nourishment for other people." My memo shorthand didn't give this crafter of words proper recognition; I wish he knew of his encouragement.

Thankful that I do not know much more, I can now praise the God who never loosens His grip on any of His children. My blonde bombshell has morphed into an exquisitely beautiful butterfly, magically bestowing a blessing wherever she lights. She handed me a Mother's Day poem several years ago, which recounts a mother's many mentoring moments and the practical and unproductive routes which her child(ren) chooses because of her godliness and wise mothering...not smothering. Children *do* what they see done, not what they hear a role-model *say*.

She found the love of her life on the baseball field, while doing a friend the favor of tagging along to a hot afternoon get-away. The night before her wedding I simply had to jot down what was dancing through my mind:

"Reggie, you will marry my little girl tomorrow, and, in the few quiet moments before the clamorous din, I covet this lull to say, "I love you!" I feel blessed to have you be a part of our family, and pray that you will always want to "come home", that you will forever feel welcomed here. Praying that Blair's love for you will deepen and grow will be pure privilege. My sweet man has been such a precious gift! May I let you know why Jack is so dear? His words to me are always soft and caring, His actions are gentle, and I feel that he truly cherishes me. Even when he thinks, "She's lost her mind", he listens and doesn't condemn. Reggie, I've lived with two men, and there is no comparison to the marriage atmosphere. Be her soul-mate; nourish her heart. Touch her often and unexpectedly. Advice I gleaned from the radio is faultless: Never tell her anything at ten o'clock at night that you haven't told her before ten in the morning in the kitchen. (Tony Evans) Hold her; kiss her often. Blair will be a loving devoted wife if you rise and bless her with your love. Read Proverbs 31:28-31.

Find a spirit-filled church in which you can worship together and fellowship with like-minded couples. My prayer is that you both will allow Him to be mighty in your marriage to use your tent bodies as He sees fit.

I am going to share a very intimate moment between Jack and me. I began to cry last night in bed, and Jack held me close. "Oh, how I wish my daddy was here to see how beautiful she is...in every way, for it was only a few days between the time I told him I was carrying this child that he left us." He tenderly responded,

"I wish your daddy were here, too to see how beautiful YOU are!" I love that man!

Thank you for asking her to marry you; I am believing in advance that one day the reverse tender testimony on her lips will intimate nothing but respect and affirmation for her husband."

We bloomed in Mississippi for eight years until we sensed His cloud over us drifting toward another horizon. Riddles without answers. Perplexing statements. Baffling matters of blame games. Enigmatical circumstances. Inexplicable events on the front end only make sense when seen in the rear view mirror. One day an accounting manager in an automotive warehouse. The next day unemployed. One day a cost account in an automotive manufacturing plant. The next day roofing houses. One day a farmhouse sold. The next day 1003 miles away in seminary. One Thursday an administrative pastor. By Friday idle and empty.

Psalm 23 promises, "Only goodness and mercy will pursue me all the days of my life." (v 6, HCSB) While I think I am relentlessly chasing life, it's really the blessed life that is hounding me. We often do not *feel* His presence, so surmise that Abba must have taken a vacation; however, by abiding in the Vine, we are most assuredly treated to a plump piece of sweet delicacy: the treasure of the warm embrace and encouragement of fellow Vine dwellers.

Monday morning. Jack was *Home Alone*. Day One. The Lord chose to wait 'til midnight in Texas to direct our path, but this time He decided He'd show up while the dew was still on the ground. The phone rang. Jack heard a strange voice ask him if he would be interested in interviewing for a new church position in Tennessee! "How did you...?" Sitting in stunned amazement, he realized that our pastor from newly-wed days had relocated to this town as area director of missions and had handed the church Jack's name the previous September.

"When do you,,,."

"How would February 28 work for you?"

February 28. The exact date ten years earlier that Jack had surrendered to His call to the ministry in a rental house on *Vista* Drive in North Carolina. The dictionary relays that *vista* is a view seen through a long passage, or a comprehensive mental view of a series of remembered or anticipated events. But we know that *vista* truly means: "Taste and see that the Lord is good."

12

...and Off He Steamed to the Roundhouse

Hattiesburg was to be HOME no longer. The night that Clarksville called to issue our invitation to return to Tennessee, all our children and grandchildren were gathered around us in a condo at Disneyworld. "Some people are related, some connected. Some people share the same space, some the same heart. Some people live in proximity, some in intimacy."[27] We were all of_the above that spring break night. Dancing the Jehovah Jireh on our beds, we were all little children, hand-in-hand around the throne. We were going HOME to Rocky Top.

Time to pack and purge....again. "Every mother has a treasure box of bonnets, blankets, trinkets, and toys, if not hidden in a closet or attic, then tucked away in a corner of her heart."[28] The opening lines of *Mary's Treasure Box* re-decorated my own heart as I pondered the railroad tracks of circumstances of the last eight years that we had called Mississippi HOME. In this fictional re-creation, Mary's grand-daughter Sarah had come to visit her. Pulling the treasure box off the shelf, Sarah asked Mary to re-tell the familiar story. They remove manger straw, sheep's wool, a tiny flute, swaddling cloth, a gold bracelet, sweet frankincense, and a vial of myrrh. Carefully, cautiously running her fingers over each item, Mary re-calls myriad memories, some overwhelmingly thrilling but some utterly devastating (only to the untrained eye).

Luke 2:19 (NASB) records the deep thoughts of one mother: "Mary treasured up all these things and pondered them in her heart." Ponder: sumballo. To put one thing with another in considering circumstances.[29] As women we are hard-wired to nurture, to hold onto, to take each building block and build a castle. Every single happening deliberately stacks on top of the last episode. Each puzzle piece has another near-by that fits in place perfectly.

As mother of five, my treasure box is an over- stuffed suitcase, brimming with items placed there through tears of joy and with pain and brokenness. Broken: "How, O Lord, how could You take my car away from me? How do You expect me to get to work?

"Why, Lord, why must You jerk every man away from me that I've ever loved? My daddy, a husband, two sons way too early?"

And a deep tender voice: **"I AM not through with you yet!"** Scars come only through wounds. Wounds come only *in* battles. Victories come only *by* battles. There is no other way.

But looking backwards I am awed at how my Lord has carried out His plans for and through me even when I've kicked and screamed and begged Him to "Let it go, let it go." He loved me too much to let me cheat myself of something marvelous for me and my family.

Purging is difficult work. It's not the endearment of an old tin cracker box or "Let's Be Neighbors" bread sign that you found while junkin' with your mother. Not the charm of the stiff tulle dress, crooked halo, and styrofoam smile pasted on an angel who came to brighten your first Christmas Day, given by your beloved grandmother Baba. Not the lure of numerous hand-made and lovingly presented child-crafted trinkets. Not the heart-shaped rock found by two young boys on a Florida beach, along with their note: "We love youl. Youl are the best parents in the wurld." The journey in "going HOME" had us stopping at many depots; various stations offered dirty, dingy, deserted menus, but, even in the unappealing, we spied ideal, immaculate, and inviting secrets.

The boys had lost their Chelsea, the only dog that they had ever known, the previous Thanksgiving, so Jack surmised that it would appease their sadness at having to move if they had a new puppy. Being in sixth and ninth grades, moving presented a world of "problems"; in "helping us" pack, Sable's little wet nose showered us with needed affection.

Someone did come along who wanted to love our house, and we quickly discovered one in Clarksville that had our names engraved on its depot door. These rudimental, but revolving roundhouse tracks would guide us into advancing adventures. Yes, our possessions would cram themselves in a moving van. Again. Tennessee to North Carolina to Texas to Mississippi and back HOME again. All the while each treasure bent its will to our craziness, as they wondered where they would be unpacked next.

Abba sat at His easel long before this day arrived, dabbing His brush in copious colors, pondering over His next stroke of love.

Royal purple - majestic robes of righteousness.

Yellow - dancing in the Sonshine, praising Him for His faithfulness.

Red - fiery trials, bloody messes.

Brown - seasons of abiding, awaiting hope.

Green - blooming, growing, flourishing.

Black - darkness.

Blue - sky full of joy, refreshment.

White - new beginnings, purity.

Just like a master weaver, He commits himself to a masterpiece - a poema.[30] God saves only by His special favor to us: a gift He individually and carefully wraps. "...lest anyone can boast. For we are His *workmanship*, created in Christ Jesus for good works, which God prepared beforehand that we should walk in them." Eph 2:9-10, NKJ.

Parallel train tracks. Coming and going. A battle here. A defeat there. A battle here. A victory there. Wilderness to abundance. Desert to oasis. Seed kernel to flower. Day by day. Another opportunity given to play the role of the seed. Roll around the small speck in my hand. Look at our lives, Lord. The fruit that we eat comes out of that small seed, placed in soil, rained upon, and warmed by the sunshine. For a seed to reproduce, it must come totally undone. The shell breaks, the seed's contents turn inside out, and it totally transfigures.

I have *so often* diligently sought to grow by my own efforts. Show my strength. DIY. I will do this if it kills me. Appear to have it all together. But the seed cracks in the dark earth. Placing a seed undercover in solitude is the *only* formula for growth. Placing myself under His wings in quietness is His lesson plan for my development. How often I have wrestled, fretted, striven in my own stubbornness! The seed pod fell from the flower in Tennessee, squiggling and wiggling, and unbending. Weary of the struggle, it would soon begin to dawn on me that the development of the hidden divine life is just like we see with our eyes as we commence into spring. No special effort needed. Just plant myself in the soil of the Word, abide in the rain of troubles, soak up the warmth of the sunshine, and rest. "For the sun meets not the springing bud that stretches toward Him with half that certainty as God, the Source of all good, communicates Himself to the soul that longs to partake of Him."[31]

13

...With Silver Bells and Cockle Shells

After a three week assignment in a tiny one bedroom apartment with a new puppy, and, after the fiasco of her devouring a son's birthday cake, we moved on to station ourselves in the Chris Drive Depot, tearing out walls, laying wood floors, and building our nest.

I woke up early one morn thinking about Psalm 103. "As high as the heavens are above the earth, so great is His lovingkindness is to those who fear Him. Just as a father has compassion on his children, so He has compassion on those who fear Him. Our days are like grass; as a flower of the field, so we flourish, but, when the wind passes, it is no more." verses 11,13,15-16, NASB.

Before the daylight peaked on the horizon, I sat enamored by the shamrock at the window, with its leaves tightly folded and drooping, as if kneeling in prayer in the dark. The morning sun soon beckoned with its teasing warmth, and chattering birds rent the darkness with welcoming choruses. The shamrock leaves flung open as their spindly stems reached out to grab the Hand of the One who ushers in the morning Light. Three leaves in one - Father, Son, and Holy Spirit - whispered my soul awake to the day's offering, unknown to me yet but already prepared for me by the One who never sleeps.

Dark to daylight. We are swaddled and tucked in nightly in His blanket, so that we His children can enjoy sweet fellowship with Him as the Son rises. How will You use me today to give Light to the dark?

Showers to Sonshine. "...and he will be like a tree firmly planted by streams of water, which yields its fruit in its season, and its leaf does not wither; and in whatever he does he prospers." Psalm 1:3, NASB.

Bulb to buttercup. Planted in the fertile soil of His care and watered by His Word to become a flourishing flower, might I be used to attract or encourage a winter weary soul before the wind passes and I am no more?

Vanity to victory. Fleshly strivings blown away by His wind become an offering of eternal value. His Life breathed into a closed-up, drooping child today because He whispered my spirit awake, threw off the warm covers of comfort, and allowed me the privilege of waiting for His Sonshine's offering, and subsequent assignment.

Roundhouse: a circular building with a turntable in its middle, used for switching locomotives and to house weary wheels. Clarksville's Chris Drive Depot offered rest to our souls through many analogous anecdotal episodes.

Roundhouse track #1 led me straight to amazing discoveries of His fingers actively working as He bent over His loom intricately weaving His strategies for a blossom to unfold from this seedpod. Eight years before this unfurling I came across a book by Susan Hunt entitled *Spiritual Mothering*. Enamored with the possibility that I could actually use my journey to help young women, I feasted on Titus 2.

A class had been offered previously in another church setting, but I guess I was expecting my ego to be inflated by visible lines of "success". Forgetting that God is the aggressor in the realm of spiritual evolution, I somewhat withered into a pity party of rejection. Ouch.

But, now, after eight years of shelf-sitting, the mentoring mandate was resurrected in my heart. The church pastor sent me to the missions pastor. Cowering in a possible second "defeat", I was greeted with an invitation to attend the Women's Ministry lead team that very night to present my desire. "I will email the director that you are coming." Arriving at the meeting with satchel in hand, I was greeted warmly; the ladies prayed with unction, praising and interceding, and laying out needs. Included in the supplications was the mentoring ministry. After a planning session, the director asked if I had anything to share from my sated satchel. Thanking them for including me at such short notice at the pastor's request, I was stopped short. "No one has contacted us" was the consensus of the group.

"So...you don't know why I am here?" A trifle confused, I extracted my goodies and began to share, cautiously fearing I would be met with the shuffling feet of sheer fitfulness but praying, however, to spy a "yes" face somewhere. In the quietness, suddenly tears. Springing out of her chair, one lady danced, "Look at these goose-bumps, ya'll!"

Thank You for listening, Lord! Hearing *about* Your mercy is not equal to *knowing* You and Your rain of mercies. Lord, reign on, for my parched soul has truly beautifully been refreshed!

I witnessed true worship. And He graced me. "You did not choose Me, but I chose you and appointed you that you should go and bear fruit and that your fruit should remain (last), that whatever you ask the Father in My name He may give you." Jesus in John 15:16, NKJ.

Like Jesus' mother Mary moved on a see-saw of emotions-up, down, up, down - I sat in the throne room being the answer to someone else's prayer, but totally inadequate and humiliated over this audience with the King. A whisper shouted in my ear, "Remember when you were agog that your pastor's prayers were hindered because you needed help? You begged Me to reimburse him. Here it is!"

Situated on the north side of Clarksville sat Fort Campbell Army Post, and soldiers - husbands and daddies - would soon bid tearful good-byes to their loved ones. The war in Iraq was calling hoards of our own men to defend our land by putting their lives on the line.

Notices were included in the church bulletins and mail-outs were post marked: Heart to Heart would be introduced and explained. "Lord, we have seen Your hand. Please send just a few ladies who would be willing to share their lives and a few more who need a special touch of lovely maturity." The chapel could not contain all the eager faces who showed up hungry for a godly companion...and those surrendered sweet ones who were willing to love on someone else's daughter.

"How can I do this, Lord? I don't have a clue. I'm overwhelmed. Scared. Inadequate...."

"You are right where I AM wants you to be! Be still and watch Me."

"Yes, Lord, yes."

Now, some twelve years later, two faces especially are pasted in my mind's eye, as if I had just extended my arms out yesterday. Paula and Jaime. Overcome with emotion. Weeping that someone somewhere cared. At the end of the evening, we had too many for one person to possibly tend to properly, so prayers were lifted heavenward for another facilitator. Is it hard to believe that the number of mentees was almost equal to the number of mentors? M and Ms - how sweet you are!

Two full classes! Every week for the next twelve weeks, we studied God's Word, encouraged and equipped each other, and grew in the knowledge of how to glorify God. The ladies dismissed each week paired with a different partner, sent out on a mission to fellowship and minister. A list of all church families was divided up. M and Ms began to pray for and even write notes to their assigned families. "Oh, what perfect timing" testimonies we received as a return for our investment. Widows and shut-ins were visited.

Super Saturday classes taught gardening, knitting, meal planning, organization skills, card making, and healthy cooking. Encouraging notes were written to the pastors and deacons. Testimonies on forgiveness broke our hearts. Widows shared ways in which we could comfort newly grieving ladies.

Oh, how I am grateful for Abba's touch on Susan Hunt and the wisdom she imparted. God wove an exquisitely gorgeous golden thread into my blanket of blessings.

When it came time for our cocoon to fall from the branch, the day I had come to dread, the separating was made delectably breath-taking. Knowing that I would ultimately be responsible for the final pairing of M and Ms was like abiding after an earthquake, knowing that a tsunami was extremely probable. However, opening the final response cards left me agog; almost unanimously the ladies had already chosen...no, God had chosen...them to be together.

A young woman unsuccessfully desiring pregnancy paired with another one who had had trouble conceiving. One whose marriage was treading water paired with one who had journeyed down that path. One who needed a nurturing mama with an encourager. A teacher whose mentor came weekly, without fail, to read to and love on her students. The relationships formed more than a decade ago are still as Energizer bunny-strong, even though, more often than not, many miles separate the ladies. Military wives move, like me, multiple times. But knowing that these young women, who have shown a desire to live for God's glory, are living out His will for them from one corner of the world to another, completely overshadowed my sorrow at our departure. I plan on having a huge tea party with them all in glory!

From there, He led us to another group willing to begin again. From this second season, He raised up a godly friend who lifted Heart to Heart to another tableland. Becky. Elegant but natural. Cultured but ingenuous. Accomplished but imaginative. Loved the Lord and opened up her home for weekly three hour sessions. Our church provided childcare.

Hour #1: Bible study, expanding on the seven mandates in Titus 2 (love your husbands, love your children, live wisely, be pure, take care of the home, do good, be submissive to husbands).

Hour #2: Cooking in the kitchen

Hour# 3: Lunch.

Becky instructed the moms on meal planning, making bread, decorating cookies (by Carol), cooking once for multiple meals, healthy food selection, good snacking, etc. As we were encircled in her kitchen one week, one of the mothers started clapping excitedly; she exclaimed, "I am leaving here and buying a kitchen table, so that we can gather around and pray like we do here and talk together as a family." What had been so simple and a "given" for us, was such a novelty for another, who allowed the TV to be the supper facilitator. Glory be.

Carol, the master cookie decorator, was another sweet benefit of our stint at Becky's. The Lord glued us together in an endearing manner. Fourteen years my junior, she and I both needed what the other could share freely. She had a zeal for cooking, a real Betty Crocker; I loved re-purposing "junk". Her front porch housed the most gorgeous plants; I had trouble keeping a cactus alive. She ingeniously encouraged her four children (all four birthed within five years); I found caring for children's mothers enamoring.

The table had been set and hospitality skills were taught. The table decorations matched the lesson plan for the day, but very simply done. For loving husbands, we had a sports theme by pulling out items from children's bedrooms that were readily available. Old toys and books were placed on a sled in the center of the table for loving children. Our purity session led us to an all white table.

I am indebted to another godly lady for the ideas we grabbed and ran with: Betty Huizenga in her *Apples of Gold* writings. Really, on my own, my creativity is stifled, but, as we ladies each open our hands and offer His blessings, gifts, and talents, what a party we can throw. Think about what a celebration we will enjoy at His prepared table one day. A feast of delicacies that will ravish and sate beyond imagination. Hallelujah!

This season of hearing His voice was the genesis of my growth into trusting and wholly believing that He is and that He delights in providing and protecting His children. *Anything* I imparted has been returned in more blessings than my apron can hold.

Now that I had had pleasure arrive before pain and *knew* that my God had my good growth in His heart and mind, I would be able to graduate on to other assignments. The next would prove that my faith needed the affirmation.

14

Rain Rain Go Away

Roundhouse Track #2: train departing from Chris Drive Depot. May 11, 2006. 7:11 a.m. Two boys and a husband fed, kissed, out the door. Sable, her tail thumping excitedly against the kitchen cabinet, was stationed in her usual spot waiting to be the beneficiary of a few breakfast crumbs. A morning breeze shimmied in from the screen porch and mixed with the aroma of hot coffee. Simple, ordinary, homely pleasures are golden nuggets from His hands. How I treasure that daily touch!

Sinking down into my well-worn chair on the porch with His Word ever near, I reveled in all the awakened senses that spring produces. Joyous choruses of birds. Leaves and flowers straight from heaven's storeroom. Sunshine's warm rays playing chase with corpulent clouds. Little did I realize at that moment how ominous those innocent clouds would become, darkening the shadows of this Sonlit day.

Thursday's plans unfolded without interruption; early in the afternoon supper began to be prepared, for a hurting friend needed its nourishment. Ingredients accounted for. Check. Spinach washed. Check. Bread was rising. Check. Chocolate cake's aroma adorned the air! Phone was ringing. "Could you come to the middle school? We have found something on your son that he should not have: marijuana in his back pocket." The clock read 4:11 p.m. Click. World stopped still.

The silence was deafening: my pastor husband was hospital shepherding, did not answer his phone, and thunder was shouting bad news! Rain threw darts at my racing heart as I fumbled with my keys. Winding through the subdivision to the highway, tears blocked my view of the road that lay ahead. But... with one stroke of the Painter's brush, hope was infused with Abba's sweet surprise. There, at "the end of my road", arched a most brilliantly colored rainbow! Way down in my soul, my Father echoed, "This one is JUST FOR you!" Palm Sunday's hosannas heralding Jesus' arrival were whispers compared to the anthem in my heart! Nothing else mattered.

Seeing Walker's swollen, tear-stained eyes led me straight to the cross. No matter what choices he had made, we would rise again. Not since Abba had picked me up from a mire of depression had I cast myself so utterly into the shadow of His wings. Only 11 days short of school's end! Almost one foot in the high school door. Court dates followed. A lawyer friend agreed to assist us as Walker appeared before the judge in a packed courtroom. As they stood, the judge motioned for the lawyers to step forward. After a brief conference, our attorney motioned for us to follow him. When we arrived outside the courtroom door, tears of tenderness spilled from his eyes. "I have been practicing 25 years; this has never happened to me! He dismissed the case before even hearing it! Our God is good...all the time!"

School administrative hearings followed with quite a different outcome. The gavel had been lowered. Zero tolerance. No freshman year. No more football practice or fall games. 14 years old and sentenced to a whole year at home with Mom. Whether His answer is "yes", "no", or "wait", God *knows* what He is doing. Take His "yes" answers and rejoice; take the "no" answers and praise Him! Take His silence and be strong, letting your heart take courage.

Walker did not realize what Mom already knew: Those who "sow in tears will reap with shouts of joy." Psalm 126:5, NASB. The lot was cast. My task was to model His faithfulness. We must, while weeping, sow seeds and expect to return with sheaves in our arms. And growth does not happen overnight.

May 11, 2007. 180 days of home-schooling finished. Four times he had presented himself to the county school officials to prove whether he had mastered state and local requirements in algebra, world geography, English, and physical science. **It had not been easy,** especially since he was tested on state-chosen curriculum, and we had journeyed through Bible-based curriculum. Four times Walker not only excelled academically, but Jesus had begun to mark his heart in red.

Early spring, 2008. Another year had passed, bringing its ordinary "dangers, toils, and snares". Walker opted to return to school his sophomore year. The battle scars have not faded but serve as a badge of determination. Just this morning, the breeze wafting His love and the birds chattering His songs, I noticed on the porch rag rug one lone red fabric fragment trying its best to escape from the ties that bound it. However, the cords held on, knowing if they let go, the rug would unravel. My Father has wrapped cords of love tightly around our family. How I praise Him for allowing my son the privilege of being held close during the storm. May mediocrity never satisfy Walker. May his obedience and continuous faithfulness to His Father be a tattoo on his life....and grace will lead us HOME.

After the saga was behind us, I asked Walker for his insights on the chronicle. A partial recounting of his testimony read: "Except for the memories, everything is pretty much the way it was. I have made many new friends since then, and I think I am more of a man to able to make my own decisions. I hope I can continue to grow in life and in my faith."

Remember the time you fell off your bike and got the air knocked out of you? To have gained a holy fear of the Lord and be able to see His fingerprints on one's life...pretty good yarn for a tall lanky teenager. Don't you think? Oh, count it a blessing, even a privilege, when your children fail while they are still under your protective wings. What growth potential in a parent's fertilizing the soil of a tender shoot!

Meanwhile, Qaneh was already enjoying lazy days on red Georgia clay, ministering to the boy/man across the road with her sturdiness, as she exuded her sweet spirit of acceptance and love. In a short two more years, she would have another bosom buddy, a Volunteer transplanted in Bulldog country.

She didn't deteriorate overnight. A little mold here. A leak there. A window knocked out in a yard baseball game that wasn't replaced. A strand of ivy clinging to the foundation chokes out the view. A dried-up well producing no more water. This house parallels my life, for He lives in me. When it needs tending to, Jesus is the *only* One qualified to clean it and do any major or minor remodeling, and, if I willingly open the door of my heart, He willingly and totally re-decorates it. No fixer uppers, no DIY. All re-creation.

In *Following Christ* Joe Stowell says there is no compromise. "He is Lord of all my life, or Lord of nothing. If I don't let Him in, I miss the experience of His presence. He will still take me HOME if I'm truly His, but, if I am hungry for Him, I will let Him in.[32] Revelation 3:20 (HCSB)states, "Listen! I stand at the door and knock. If anyone hears My voice and opens the door, I will come in to him and have dinner with him, and he with Me."

We who *know* Jesus are His tabernacle, His dwelling place; therefore, *we* are His house...the place He "stays", His address. In Old Testament economy, His presence was in the temple, in the Holy of Holies. But since the day the Holy Spirit arrived, 50 days after Resurrection Sunday, He is the light in His children's lives. As baby Christians, and seekers of His heart, our new nature surrenders gladly to the Carpenter's toolbox and His remodel.

But...He is not content just to slap on a fresh coat of paint and replace a light fixture. This house will be gutted: all sheetrock hammered and crushed, electrical wires slashed, plumbing pitched in the dumpster. Its bones are exposed and begin to shiver and beg for a sheepskin blanket; being unmasked isn't so much fun anymore. Herein lies our choice...we can allow this suffering for a season, believing that hearty wholesomeness is born only from painful brokenness, or we can halt the process early on and live in the decrepit, sickly, exhausted, puny, albeit familiar, predicament. Microwave mentality or delayed delight. We see in a mirror dimly now, but one day, in repentance, rest, quietness, and trust, we will see Him face to face. What a party... streamers waving; redeemed ones shouting, singing, skipping, swaying to praises! RSVP now!

15

Simple Simon Met a Pieman

Locomotive ready for departure on Roundhouse Track #3.

"There is an appointed time for everything. And there is a time for every event under heaven. All God does will last forever; there is no adding to it or taking away. God works so that people will be in awe of Him." Ecclesiastes 3:1, 14, NASB.

Mentoring to marijuana. El Shaddai. He is sovereign but nurturing. Daddy and Mama. Strong but soft. Stern but tender.

A new church staff member had been hired. However, his daughter was beginning her senior year of high school eighty miles away, so he and his family would be apart much of the next year.

Debbie and I first became acquainted during her husband's interview process. We drove around town, chatting as if reconnecting from a long absence. "When I talk to my closest female friends, I feel my soul being sunned and watered when they ask questions, drawing out the deep waters of my soul, and when they empathize, rejoicing when I rejoice, weeping when I weep."[33] The year that Debbie and I were apart, we emailed almost daily. Even though we couldn't share orally, face to face, God united our hearts, and a "cord of three strands is not easily broken." Ecclesiastes 4:12, HCSB.

Many written words were carefully weighed and measured, for we both paint portraits with a pen much more fluently than with conversation. Quiet contemplations echo messages that are endless, but quick tongues are fiery couriers.

Having many acquaintances is a fortunate fluke, perhaps even a blissful privilege, but, when one friend is presented to another straight from Abba's hand, exquisitely delivered, tied with golden ribbons, and perched on a silver tray, we are refreshed as powerfully as the gentle spring rain. "Like apples of gold in settings of silver is a word spoken in right circumstances." Proverbs 25:11, NASB. Debbie and I ate the richest of foods those twelve months. Sated we were indeed.

July 12. Jill:

The computer may be packed, but I could not resist ONE LAST thought via the wire waves that have been our umbilical cord. I feel like a child on Christmas Eve waiting for Santa but then again like a bride, knowing that one life is gone and a brand new one unfolds. Why does the past hang on like the desire to pull my baby blanket to my face...familiarity...security...saturated in word bubbles? Thank you for garrulously meandering with me, for dawdling on this see-saw of verbage.

Even though I am thrilled that you will soon be here to join your husband, I am somewhat apprehensive that God might lead us on different journeys. This year of correspondence has endeared itself to me more than I realized, because tears drip on the keyboard of scrambled letters. We have both been through fire this year; however, our clothes remain fresh, and our spirits soar to new heights, knowing not the future "What ifs...", but secure in *Who* holds our hands and hearts.

So..."Happy are the people whose strength is in You, whose hearts are set on a pilgrimage. As they pass through the Valley of Baca (Weeping), they make it a source of spring water; even the autumn rain will cover it with blessing." Psalm 84:5-6, HCSB.

Together we travel; the Lord will grant us undivided hearts to spread His aroma wherever He plants us.

July 13. Debbie:

What a sweet inspiration you have become! Thank you for your timely reminders of His faithfulness. I would hope the Lord will continue to water our friendship like spring bouquet that bursts to life with the benefit of tender breezes and warm sunshine.

Speaking of baby blankets, as we were unpacking boxes from the attic tonight, I found a box of our babies' clothing-including Nathan's baby blanket. I did just that-pulled it to my face just to try to capture the baby scent of him among the overloved and faded threads...yes, it is familiarity, security, a longing to return to the days of newborn wonder...It may be God's reminding us that one day in the future today will be the day we long to recapture years from now-the pencil marks on the pantry door recording how tall our children have grown through the years, the tire swing and the treehouse in the backyard now silent of squeals of laughter, the flower box backdrop for preteen and teen formal dates, snowy winter mornings with tots in footed pajamas...His marvelous blessings in each chapter of our wondrous book called life...

I believe that I have shared with you in honesty that I feel much less vulnerable behind the pen than in person. Therefore... if our correspondences travel across emails rather than in person, so be it. It is my prayer that, once settled, we can enjoy one on one time and share our hearts in a myriad of ways. God has used you mightily to bring peace into my life through His wooing, and for that provision and your willingness, I will ever be grateful.

I have been wondering about the determination made concerning Walker...

Almost there!

August 24. Jill (on receiving a devotional largess):

What a precious gift was hiding in my car! When I got home, Jack was near-by as I read your book note. His comment, "Boy, were you two poured out of the same mold!" brought a smile to my face, while his words seeped into the pleats of my dearest thoughts. My heart's sweetest comfort is the assurance that you deliberately pondered and acted on a desire from my message to you the week of your move.

August 28. Debbie:

Did you by chance notice the entry in the devotional yesterday? It never ceases to amaze me how the Lord can so perfectly provide both comfort and teaching in His Word in such a timely fashion. The reminder about Abraham's possessiveness was powerful for me in the backdrop of Jonathan and Sarah moving to their dorms and Bethany's upcoming wedding. I certainly would never wish to be the obstacle that prevents the blessings God has planned for them to receive. I love the illustration that only by releasing our hand from that of our children are we able to grasp His.....

August 29. Jill:

The Leaf-Chronicle this morning ran a full page color photograph of the 100th celebration of Clarksville High football. On the cover are the fourth year letter seniors for this graduating class. Taylor's coach "neglected" to include him in the picture or the write-up: the only one "forgotten". My soul had to smile: Jesus was forgotten, too. So, I picked up our book and retreated to the coolness and the quietness of the screened porch..."your mind goes off on tangents from its Holy Center." His word tells us to take every thought captive to the mind of Christ, and my mind, divided between huffiness and happiness, spied the rag rug in front of me. "Don't you know that you are a temple of the Living God?" As I gazed on many pieces of that tattered rug begging to escape, I realized that that was exactly what I was doing.

But Jesus will not let me go. The cords of His love will never snap. And you are the third strand in that strong braid that Solomon lays out for us. I would have never realized that peace this morning if Sarah Young's musings in *Jesus Calling* had not been there; in essence, your friendship delivered Him to me. How can we say thanks? C. S. Lewis once stated, "God gives His gifts where He finds vessels empty enough to receive them." He gives the healing and grace our hearts always hunger for...

August 30. Debbie:

On our next coffee fellowship, I will share with you about Jonathan's senior year on the basketball team. It still hurts when I think about it, but it developed a character and integrity that he may not otherwise have experienced, so I trust that the Lord worked through it in spite of circumstances. Almost every time I read your emails, I am convinced you need to write for publication. Have you ever considered it? Just wondering...

December 7. Jill:

Oh, dear friend, Taylor was not recognized in August, and I was hurt; but tonight at the football award ceremony, he was rewarded for his diligence and commitment to the team by receiving the prestigious Leadership Award and a scholarship. Hurt pivoted into indignation. The scholarship benefactor, openly hurdled crass words in his speech, full of obese audacity.

The initial words, "Greatness is measured by one's ability to inspire others..." had danced in my mind's eye since his freshman year, thinking how precious it would be, as a parent, to be rewarded by one's son being found worthy to receive this recognition. Leadership, attitude, encourager....higher plane characteristics.

"The wise shall inherit glory, but shame shall be the legacy of fools." Proverbs 3:35, NKJ. When given the privilege of ministering to young men, one must realize that with honor comes great responsibility. While he spoke tonight, the auditorium clothed itself in shame. I found myself praying Taylor's name would *not* be called, for the model of mentoring was being blasphemed. Jack and I have tried to teach our children to be models of integrity and sound speech that cannot be censored. The award tonight was profaned and its value cheapened. The filthy rags of garbage placed in those young men's minds can never be washed clean. Why did no coach rise up for righteousness?

"My son, do not forget my (wisdom's) law, but let your heart keep my commands; for length of days and long life and peace they will add to you." Proverbs 3:1-2, NKJ.

What a fiasco, a black dot of permanent indelibility. Dead. Without possible resurrection.

My manila folders brim over with letters, words, and figures, all bubbled forth from a mind's liquid water-colors. Just symbols pasted together with heartstrings and yet pieces of the scraps of lives. Clean up. Clean up. Everybody do your part. "Clean up, clean up" we teachers and mothers sing as the children pitch in and help. Help gather up snippets of daily lives. Mutual sympathies and empathies. Arms entwined in struggles, but arms raised in victories. Participating in the stuff of the commonalities of daily circumstances.

"We look forward to Thursday night; the guys have said 'No women in the basement', but we may have a party to crash."

Shared physical and spiritual needs for child's wedding.

"Please pray for ____; her mama has cancer."

"How about the craft fair on Friday?"

Commiserating when children's romantic break-ups tear asunder.

Arranging tea parties with several widows.

"How long will you be in Louisville caring for your mom? I will see that Ron and his mother get food."

Youth retreat food coordination.

In an era of microwave disclosures, communal facebook messages between a copious sum of friends, and innumerable pop-ups percolating pleas of consideration to sate ego-agendas, is there any wonder why we feel so drained? The massage parlors are glutted with exorcism offerings for achy tense bodies. Our children have dance practice, karate, ball games, gymnastics, and then week-ends are plump with travel teams and soccer games.

Disposable containers and throw-away diapers catch dirty poop; do I initiate conversations and linger long enough to listen or do I throw out my husband's and children's comments? How welcoming am I to nightly homecomings and early morning exits? Is the atmosphere friendly enough to allow vulnerability without my scowling? Is the laundry of life washed and hung in the sunshine to air-dry, or do we add cologne to sweaty clothes, hoping to make it another day without confrontation? Often frivolous conversations are an old toothbrush, discarded to be a scrub brush, but the bristles are so disheveled that they are good for purifying no stain at all.

What a Jesus we have in a friend. Interactions loiter, never to be deleted. The 'escape' and 'backspace' buttons can't erase tears and laughter. E-bay and Google don't hold a candle to the smile and touch of a loved one. Highlight the times of contagious enthusiasm. Bold the text of children's "I love you" messages. Begin a multi-level list of the small ways that joy seeps into the day. Cut and re-paste only the large fonts of A to Z acts of faithfulness.

Logos, or icons, on the screen saver tell us where to locate items that we deem important, places we click to take us on our chosen adventure.

LOGOS – the Word – the expression of God's thoughts through His Son. Jesus embodied all His Father's treasures of divine wisdom and expressed the inmost nature of God Himself.[34] Logos or LOGOS. It's a choice. Flesh or spirit. Law or grace. Where is my heart?

16

There Was an Old Woman Tossed Up in a Basket

Turntable train on Track #4 stoking up its engine.

August 11, 2009. The first day of Walker's senior year! The friends, football, and fun had waited on him, and the Lord had multiplied the time that the locusts had eaten up. Senior boys often came to lounge in our basement man-cave, ate heartedly, and watched sport reruns of games past, as they anticipated a fall filled with fellowship and plays not yet made. The aroma in this mother's mind, however, was not of locker rooms but of powder puffs...those given by another 18 year old child of hers, who in December,1991, in the middle of his senior year, married his love and then would soon watch his baby daughter birth a tender place in his immature heart. On John's wedding day, I waddled down the aisle two months shy of birthing Walker, and his bride only several months away from cradling their Alyssa.

So...at the age of 42, I, like Sarah (even though she had 50 years on me), laughed over what was to be a paradox of sorts. This school year, I host in my heart the unique overwhelming experience of watching Walker, my last born of five children, dig down his last roots here and then take wing to the world. But, alas, my husband and I also offer hospitality to another special senior: our granddaughter Alyssa.

Her father knew at age eleven that his gifts were in the construction field. He built a shed in our backyard, only to be told when we moved, that it was on neighbor's property. John has moved, too, from sheds to large commercial structures, from home's laughter and tears to deafening silence in an extended-stay motel. A shed easily moved a few feet, but a heart tore across the miles. Like Mary, I have had to ponder many strange happenings; both good and bad travel on the same worn trail. God shows up in the uniqueness of each of our circumstances. His planning is puzzling to the immature in faith but an affirmation of His provision to the more seasoned.

John is my first born. Thirty-six years young in age, but a pile of missed memories have begun to mound up like dirty laundry. Where did all the pig-tails, T-ball games, school programs, family farm fun, rodeo and 4H programs, and her presidential presentation at the high school agriculture banquet go? One day John will realize that God wastes nothing. The shiny gold seed falls into the cold black earth only to fall apart, as it lies patiently for the blossom. Alyssa's love of the farm *will* show her dad that the "farmer waits for the precious fruit of the earth, and He has patience for it until it receives the early and late rain." James 5:7, HCSB.

Rain brings rainbows, and His mysteries reveal His ways. Tragedy is the cue card for triumph. Expulsion brings exposure. No freshman year for Walker, but He Himself showed up to teach. Fatherhood for an 18 year old John, but He brought softness with Alyssa. John's story has been written on my heart for a much longer season, as intoxicatingly addicting as the aroma of an infant's newness. My child and my grandchild will both stand up to graduate from high school this May!

On the stage of life they both anticipate a world that may or may not meet their expectations. I will welcome hope. John's long gaze into a dim mirror will clear to reflect the gaze of a faithful Father. Alyssa is a farm girl; she plants, waters, and dotes over hidden life. She physically tends to birthing calves, and the Spirit is hovering over another prospective birth, one not seen by the eye.

May 10, 2010. Two grandparents watch a beautiful young lady gracefully flow across her commencement stage in high heels. She may be dreaming of boots and jeans, but work clothes must wait for tomorrow, after the celebration of new life.

May 25, 2010. On the eve of Alyssa's 18th birthday, two parents glow with pride when a tall slender son saunters across his divide. His handsome profile reminds his parents that the scars from 15 skin surgeries have faded in the spotlight of His care.

Seen walking in the shadow of His wings, a child and a grandchild will shift their black tassels toward the golden Son, and this child will proudly reflect the beauty of His grace and mercy. And I will smile.

17

This Little Piggy Stays HOME

Roundhouse locomotive on track #5: Last train of the evening. All aboard.

Once again the turntable revolves to release its locomotive down the track toward another depot. In God's economy it will go straight to its designated destination taking no detours, but delivering its cargo on time and intact.

Women are charged with generating a welcoming ambience to the home. Our ingenious talents to nurture and infuse others with courage (we also can slam a child's spirit when not living in the Spirit) gives the little seeds freedom to burst forth, to blossom into who God created them to be, to bloom and stretch toward the Son. Son or searing sun...is it worth a consistent quiet time?

Of all the journeys I have traveled, nothing compares to this ongoing saga. Exodus 33:14 (NASB): "My presence will go with you, and I will give you rest." Moses responded, "If Your presence does not go with us, don't lead us up from here. How will it be known that I and Your people have found favor in Your sight unless You go with us? I and Your people will be distinguished by this from all the other people on the face of the earth." The Lord answered, "I will do this very thing you have asked, for you have found favor in My sight, and I *know you by name.*"

If not for this assurance and the plea in Psalm 27, "I would have despaired unless I had believed that I would see the goodness of the Lord in the land of the living. Wait for the Lord; be strong and take courage. Wait!" v. 13-14, NASB.

This saga has been brewing for over 30 years. I have been crushed by my mistakes. I am imprisoned in a torture of my own making. Drowning in a deep vortex of regret. Gluttonous to suppress how I've starved those I was meant to love.

Divorce is no picnic... but *to leave your children....* A self-inflicted wound? Yes, as deadly as the real bullet that Daddy used to end his misery. My scab has been scraped off many times; has released venom with each tearing; and cowers down again, holding its breath, hoping it heals before the next skirmish.

Boys 12 and 14. New husband. New job 465 miles down the road. Brand new baby three days old, but I fly off. Daddy left. Mama left.

Qaneh tried to weather her storm but now is a hollow shell, only four-tenths of a mile from my HOME. Never a light on in the dark. Never a child playing in the yard. The old trusty rusty tractor laments for the farmer who never darkens the barn door. The snow tries to cover it all with its pristine whiteness, but there is still rottenness under its cloak of purity.

"HOME is where memories and possessions become one. Laughter shared and tears consoled are instantly recalled with the hum of the furnace and smells from the kitchen. Secret places and hidden emotions are all safely tucked away but within reach. Every object speaks to your personality, and all the truly important people in your life have shared this sanctuary. Love is the single ingredient that transforms your dwelling into a HOME."[35]

"By allowing vulnerable experiences in quiet and rest, you become a person who makes every context a safe place. Your life becomes shelter, whether giving good-night kisses to a child or listening to the secret dreams of a spouse."[36]

Thirty years is a spacious span of days but really only yesterday. Yes, consequences of sin come courting and even marry us, but I missed two children's high school graduations, a God and Country Boy Scout award ceremony, the birth of more than one grandchild, the haunting accusations (mostly from within) that I had replaced my family.

"If I should say, 'Lord, my foot has slipped', Your lovingkindness will hold me up. When my anxious thoughts multiply within me, Your comforts delight my soul." Psalm 94:18-1, NASB. And Psalm 5:3 and 7 constantly, consistently waft toward heaven from my heart: "In the morning I will order my prayer to You and eagerly watch. It is by Your abundant lovingkindness that I will enter Your house." The handprints of each of *my* children and grandchildren have been tenderly placed in the Potter's hands: the turning of the wheel by His feet, the water of the Holy Spirit, the clay that lies limp and malleable in His big El Shaddai hands. Abba awaits our choice as a mannequin's clothing awaits a savvy shopper.

The night before son #3 left for college, we gathered before supper to pray. Holding my son's hand with the right hand and my sweet man's hand with the left, I was overcome with emotion. While the size of a man's hand, Taylor's grasp was smooth and "immature". Jack's hand, made plump with scars from woodworking, yard tending, and even age, were rough; however, their grip felt tender and gave me the security of being protected and cared for. Dwelling in softness but resting in strength.

Faith is just that: dwelling in the softness of His love but resting in the strength of His yoke. All things... *all things...* all things He uses to woo each one of us... no matter what... no matter what happens. We stand before the Master Tailor to be fitted with the finest cloth and exact measurements.

The inexorable fact is: God is *not* in a hurry! He may *appear* to be delayed to us slow learners, but He never has and never will be late for a performance. It's already been choreographed, rehearsed, designed, and orchestrated. I believe He will withhold no good thing if I remain faithful and immovable in my prayers and trust. No strength to fix it! The only one to rescue the renovation is its Creator, not me! From the inside out. The seemingly unbelievable is actually true. God works backwards from the ways of the world. The way up is down. The fruit pit sleeps in darkness. The life deep inside is encased in hardness and can't get out, so why kick against the goads? Inside in the sanctuary, life is clothed with blackness. But it s-l-o-w-l-y begins to soften, so that the embryo can be fed. DIY girls must learn to repent and rest before the Holy Spirit can nourish them.

I am being tutored day by day, month by month, to trust Him for what I cannot do myself – and *never* could, and I am fully expecting Him to act "on behalf of those who love Him."

"Just satisfy me in the morning, Lord, with Your lovingkindness, that I may sing for joy and be glad all my days." Psalm 90:14, NASB.

"Light is sown like seed for the righteous." Psalm 97:11, NASB. One day at a time, sweet Jesus.

18

So Come Little Children...

cuddle closer to me in your dainty white nightcap and gown, and I'll rock you away to that Sugar-Plum Tree in the garden of Shut-Eye Town.[37]

There are no more flickering lights in the windows, summoning family to come in for rest and comfort. No more bikes lean on the front steps, signaling a child at play who needed a boo-boo kissed. There are no more fires warming cold toes or afghans to warm hearts. The only flowers blooming are plastic buttercups planted under the porch column by a grandchild craving stale by-gone memories to glow afresh. The creaky wooden floors gape open in spots and can't, therefore, support the laughter of little children. No more baking bread beckoning the men folks to supper. No more playful puppies howling at the deer grazing out by the barn. No more farm catalogs delivered to a mailbox for daddy to muse over.

The roof leaks. The absent window panes allow cold harsh winds to abide with the rodents living within. Vines have choked her neck. Qaneh aches with arthritis, yet she smiles at me as I wave while busily running errands. She has become rich by giving her all. Every opportunity she was afforded was an occasion to acquiesce with her assignment – to give a sincere cordial welcome to all who called her "HOME".

I know because I am her friend. We've had afternoon walks together. Her grandson recounted to me that she still gives him comfort, although all the dear ones that loved him there are long gone. His mom and dad divorced when he was a youngster, so in the refuge of Qaneh's wings he discovered refuge with Grandma and Grandpa.

There are days when Qaneh and I just sit and chat, not to enjoy a pity party but to share life. Yes, our eyes need reading glasses, our skin sags, and we have strange pangs in our joints. It took many years to acquire this crown. The peculiar paradox of God's paths. The way up is down. The way in is out. Procuring contentment emerges only through befriending loneliness. No mending is required until first something has been smashed and broken. Pristine facades arise from hackneyed mediocrity. Last is first. Finding arrives only after losing.

But neither of us tryst to whine or complain but just to share a cup of tea and koinonia. In sweet fellowship we ponder how good God has been. Like the Velveteen Rabbit we both have become REAL, but only because the Father has loved us to pieces by keepin' on keepin' on with us. We fall down; we get up. Yes, I voted for His salvation, but it took an eon for Him to dismantle this DIY girl one brick at a time. He *did* fell Jericho with one mighty roar, but He raises up one block at a time. Until each of us is slathered with the cement of His learning, He will try, and try again, lovingly and patiently. How often I *smiled* at salvation but kept on licking that ice cream cone of lust. I called on my Santa Claus with my wish list. I continually inserted coins into the vending machine and pulled on the lever of favorite fleshly desires. I often still do, but I earnestly seek to recognize the futility of purchasing combustible material. Coming again across a sliver of torn paper, I rehearse, "The old nature has no good; the new nature has no power", and this truth commenced to allow me to release my grip on my cleaning rag. Often we take too lightly the fact that we are sinners. SIN is a piece of lint to be dusted away. Oh, no, it is an immovable boulder, our old nature. A person who is not as good, as holy, as pure as God is not acceptable to Him, only because of His innate nature. He can't, He shouldn't, He couldn't, He wouldn't; He is utterly unable to embrace even one thought or gesture of obscenity or pollution. "There is none righteous, not even one." Romans 3:10, NASB. "The heart is more deceitful than anything and is desperately (incurably) sick." Jeremiah 17:9, NASB. We are wholly, totally, entirely, collectively spiritually ignorant. No blame can we place on poor circumstances or lack of opportunity, for no one wants to know, to understand, nor to obey God. Salvation is seen, not as a blessing, but a threat to our everyday activities.

We actually go AWOL and desert Him, all the while thinking we can throw a godly kiss His way, so He will know that we think about Him every now and then. Our actions seem right to us, but, all the while, we determinately, avidly head straight in to the enemy camp. Sin is a debt, a poison, a sting, a kudzu, a thief. Every child born is a little savage; we want our own way, and we want it now. Leave a child to his own ways, and the ego will win without fail. Bursting forth in "immorality, impurity, sensuality, idolatry, sorcery, enmities, strife, jealously, outbursts of anger, disputes, dissensions, factions, envying, drunkenness, carousing", one will not "practice these things and inherit the kingdom of God". Galatians 5:19-22, NASB. SIN will dig our grave for us. The "I" is smack in the middle of all rebellion.

No, we didn't ask to be born. We didn't ask for this innate filthy nature. But God didn't create us to be born that way either! I delight as I listen to the melodious chorus that my grandchildren repeat with folded hands, "God is great, God is good, and we thank Him for our food." He IS GREAT! He IS GOOD! And in Genesis...in the beginning of time...we hear the story of creation. For five days He created light; the sky; the earth; plants, fruit trees, and seeds; the sun, moon, and stars; creatures, birds, livestock, and wildlife. It was all good and pleased Him.

Then He said, "Let Us (Himself, Jesus, and the Holy Spirit) make man in Our image, according to our likeness. They (men) will rule the fish, birds, livestock, and all creatures." Genesis 1:26, NASB. And it was **very** good! It was perfect! It was Eden! It was Paradise itself! It was the way it ought to be, created to be...

Well, what happened? Love isn't love until one gives it away; Abba (a daddy with great tenderness and compassion) allowed Adam and Eve (just as He does us) the privilege, the favor, the liberty of **choosing** to love. If we had no choice, we would be robots; and mechanical toys are "very superior, and look down on everyone else; they are full of modern ideas, and pretend they are REAL."[38] I don't want my children to be *made* to love me! How glorious it is, when, in pure emotion and with deep affection, they shower us with kisses and throw tiny arms around our necks.

God is a Person, too, so He relishes the delicacy of our sweet praises. This is how it should be, how He designed it to be.

What happened? With the gift of choice comes the ability to say "No" to love. Because God is the holy, righteous Creator, He has the right to be the authoritative sovereign Abba. He bestowed on Adam the *task of ruling over his creation*, but the Lord God gave him this warning: "You are free to eat from any tree of the garden, *but you must not eat* from *the* tree of the knowledge of good and evil'." One tree! That's all He asked. For "on the day you eat from it, you will certainly die!" Genesis 2:16-17, HCSB.

We must set boundaries for our own children to care for and protect them from harm. What kind of Father would He be if He didn't test our love? "Do not cross the sidewalk, for, if you do, a car will crush you!" What happens when a river overflows its banks? Even the sun rises and sets on opposite ends of the earth, but all the while staying within the ropes of its corral.

He would not be a great and good Father if He didn't judge poor choices. Poor child when Mama gives in to every whim, every tantrum. Holiness holds the line, even when we scream,

"It's not fair!" But we don't understand: we have the freedom to foul up, to sin. There can be no trust without His loving boundary-setting.

When children disobey, there are consequences that serve as a tutor. God has the responsibility and the authority to decide sin's consequences. He, as Eve's Father, adjudicated equitable significant consequences, not to punish, but to teach, to lead her back to the holiness with which He created her. "I will intensify your labor pains; you will bear children in anguish. Your desire will be for your husband, yet he will dominate you." Genesis 3:16, HCSB. How we women want the last word!

To Adam: "Because you listened to your wife's voice and ate from the tree about which I commanded you... the ground is cursed because of you. You will eat from it by means of painful labor all the days of your life. It will produce thorns and thistles for you...and you will eat bread by the sweat of your brow until you return to the ground." Genesis 3:16-19 HCSB. Paradise given and Paradise taken; choices continually consistently beckon. Will I delight in His manna or in the bread of fools?

If we had been there, we, too, would have asked, "Who is He that can instruct me?" Perfection was reduced to weeds and thorns, intimacy became enmity, war overshadowed peace, family fragrances soured into broken bridges, purity descended into immorality, praises crumbled to idolatry, worship ebbed to ego adulation. *Now we know what evil is and wish we didn't.* Now our own very nature is unworthy to burst into the throne room, for we stink like peasants.

Because of His utter perfection and purity, He was unable to take us to Himself any longer. Mama won't let her little one in the house if he's been mud-stompin' down by the pond on a hot summer's day. Whew! Rotten potatoes! Dirty sewage! Why, she'll scrub you so hard you think your skin will right off with the greasy grimy sweaty stench. Ears, between the toes, hair. What she craves is to cuddle you closely as she smothers you with kisses on the top of your head, sating herself with the delightful aroma.

If Mama is so satisfied over such a simple, fleshly moment, how many zillion times over must El Shaddai intensely eagerly crane His neck, longing to catch a glimpse of our running home to His arms. But, unlike Mama, and because of His purity, He *can't* take us to His breast until we are cleaned up – spiritually. We are just like Adam and Eve: we hurt Him, disappoint Him, take Him for granted, and think that if we work hard enough, He will welcome us. But He *can't*. Holiness cannot glue itself to sin, even if it's only a dust-bunny.

So God devised a way to buy us back, redeem us, clean us up on the inside...if we so choose Him. He loves us and craves fellowship with His children. After Adam and Eve sinned, "the Lord God made garments of skin for Adam and his wife and clothed them." Genesis 3:21, NASB. This was to cover their shame and to demonstrate that, in order for sin to be covered, a sacrifice had to be offered. His choice before Jesus' resurrection was that the blood of an unblemished animal would be shed to cover a sinner's unrighteousness, only a preview of the coming main attraction.

But He is not bound by time. His timing seems so slow, but one thousand years is as day. For the last several thousand years, He's been unfolding His grand scheme. Because God's masterpieces are painted in paradox, He called out a no-body from the middle of nowhere, a man named Abram. He asked Abram to leave his home, but He did not tell him where he'd be going, only that He'd show him, bit by bit, rule on rule. His benefits do not accrue but are meted out day by day. Sarai, his wife, was old, they had no children, but God made him an unbelievable promise: "Go forth from your country to the land I will show you; I will make you a great nation (my question: a what?), and I will bless you... and *in you* all the families of the world will be blessed." Genesis 12:1-3, NASB.

And so He began the process of buying us back, but the present remained wrapped up until the fullness of His time. He made Abram an example of how He wants to relate to us all – personally. Adam and Eve were given only one rule, but they failed. Only one request was made to Abram-to believe Him.

What exactly is this "belief"? How is it fleshed out? "To believe is to make an unqualified commitment of oneself to another in total trust, no holding back."[39] There can be no relationship without trust. God chose Abram, and He chooses us, despite all our faults, and then shows Himself strong through our weakness. Sarai was 65 and barren. How could he possibly father a nation when he couldn't even father a child? 26 years later Sarai bore their child! At 91 years young it came about, when there was humanly no other explanation but, "God did it!"

"Abram *believed* the Lord, and He credited it to him as righteousness." Genesis 15:6, HCSB. God promised to give him the land of Canaan (Israel). To seal this promise, He asked Abram to bring certain animals, which Abram cut in half and laid open. "Know for certain that your descendants *will* be strangers in a land that is not theirs, where they will be enslaved for 400 years, but *I will* also judge the nation whom they will serve; and afterward, they will come out with many possessions." And on that day the Lord made a covenant with Abram, saying, "To your descendants I have already given this land.." Genesis 15:13, 14, 18, NASB. To signify His sure promise, Abram's *name* ("exalted father") *was changed* to Abraham ("father of a multitude").

Descendant means SEED. HOLD THAT THOUGHT! (I am jubilating over this scenario! The symbols on the page cannot keep pace with beautiful thoughts dancing across my mind. I cannot give away just yet the last few thoughts of the wet ink still flowing red and dancing in my soul.) God literally passed through the animals, right in the middle of the bloody mess, with a flaming torch and smoking oven. Once again, blood was spilled to show that Abba was dead serious about being a Promise

Keeper. He will redeem us – no matter what! All He solicits in return is that we *believe Him*, that He is who He says He is, and so we can utterly trust Him. Things were looking up for Israel.

Not too long ago my daughter bore a daughter. "Mom, could you make curtains and a bedskirt for Jillian's crib?" I planned on paper, made shopping excursions on every highway within a 50 mile radius, mulled over patterns, pondered over numerous frilly designs. My fingers ran over linen, silk, polished cotton, braiding. Stripes of mint green and pink, polka-dots, vintage material and shabby chic. What joy! What blessedness! His Spirit whispered in my ear, "That's just how it is when I think about you and My preparing a place for you! I cherish every single detail of designing your life! I create every circumstance to fit together; it's all tailor-designed! One day you and I will gaze on the completed puzzle and dance!"

After God's unconditional covenant with Abraham, his great grandson Joseph did indeed end up in Egypt, sold by his brothers in a hate crime. Joseph's family multiplied into nation status in the next 400 years, but they were severely oppressed as slaves to pharaoh. The way up is down, and the Jews were exactly where God wanted them. Life's greatest opportunities are right in the midst of its most unsolvable and detestable problems. Will you believe in the Deliverer and trust Him **(on the front end)** to act on your behalf? God caused nine great catastrophies, pelting troubles on all their gods, but still pharaoh refused to release the slaves, even though Moses pleaded.

He allowed them to remain in order to show His power... that He *could* be wholly trusted. Seven times He relays His promises in Genesis 6:6-8, but only after He recounted the times He had already strongly supported them. "I will...bring you, deliver you, redeem you, take you, be your God, bring you, give you..."

Do you believe He can deliver you from the chains that hold you prisoner? Do you trust Him, even if it appears to be hopeless?

In plague #10 God told each Jewish family to kill an unblemished lamb, spread its blood over the doorposts, and have a party, feasting on the animals that had been slaughtered! How bizarre! A party? In the midst of such miserable and vexatious circumstances? Celebrate? "But we are rotting here in this wasteland!"

"Believe Me, trust Me!" In Exodus 12:12 He exclaimed, "I will pass through the land of Egypt and strike every first-born male...but when I see the blood I will **pass over** you." Exodus 12:12,13 NASB.

Once again, He showed His people His way to be rescued, saved...under the blood! Marvelous miracles had graced the Jewish nation. Would they now believe, open their hands, show their thanks, and adore their Liberator? What should have been a short journey HOME turned into a 40 year hiatus, as they wandered in circles, whining and complaining.

Why are children given rules? Isn't it because of love? To protect them, to keep them from harm, to teach them to respect others. To impart values. To model what we treasure as dear. God personally hand-wrote His commandments, His expectations for His children on stone tablets, only because of His undying faithful love for His own. He was confirming who He was and how dear this nation was to Him. His patience with this unruly group of nomads was unimaginable. But isn't He still the same with us?

Josh McDowell's mantra is: "Rules without relationship leads to rebellion." Seventy times seven we have to crawl back to Abba, but, if we truly are His and we believe His road to salvation, His arms are *always* open, and He crouches down as we run to Him, so He can swoop us up in His big strong, but tender, arms, so that He can hold us close and dance with us. He never has and never will ask for a report card on our performance. Relationships *precede* rules! Love trumps laws. Laws say, "Do this and live." Faith says, "Believe Me and live!"

Because this monstrous myriad of gypsies continued to disrespect Him, sacrifices continually had to be offered: the blood of animals sprinkled on an altar. Wonder after wonder, His nation finally made it home to heavenly Canaan.

But His children still were rebels at heart. God dispatched judges to arbitrate, prophets to predicate, and kings to regulate, but this roguish band of vagabonds continued in old sin patterns. Contrition. Docility. Dissatisfaction. Compliance. Penitence. Obedience. Remorse. Joy. Complacency. Diligence. The see-saw goes up; the see-saw comes down. But still God called them to "come HOME". Home. Not a plot to be found on the GPS, but a refuge for the heart.

In the revolving door of comings and goings, God always provided a watchman to proclaim His word. He dubbed David as king, a man after His own heart. God brought His covenant on stage once again, to verify that He was still in the business of redeeming them as a people, demonstrating to the world that He is who He says He is and that He fully intends to keep His promise to Abraham and to His people.

Through the prophet Nathan, God vowed to David, "When your days are fulfilled and you rest with your fathers, *I will* set up your seed after you, who will come from your body. II Samuel 7:12, NKJ. Your house and your kingdom shall endure before Me *forever.*" II Samuel 7:16, NASB. David did have a son Solomon who built a temple for God, but ultimately the Lord built a forever house for David through *the* Son Jesus.

Hundreds of years later, after God had given them multiple opportunities to hide themselves under His feathers, the fulfillment of prophesy over a 3000 year period came to fruition. When the time was just right, God sent His Son to earth, born of a virgin teenager and impregnated by the Holy Spirit. The New Testament ("Covenant Promises") gives the ancestry first of Joseph, Jesus' legal father, and then of His mother Mary. Both were blood descended from David, King of Judah! Matthew opens with the good news, relaying the saga of Joseph, to prove Jesus' credentials as king of the chosen nation. Dozens of Old Testament prophesies are reiterated as verification that He is the One who is the rightful king.

Then Luke traced out carefully Mary's lineage and quoted her consummated submissive reply to her Abba, one which is sated with Old Testament quotes and allusions. The four gospels then continue to advocate the truth that Jesus is the One who His father had spoken of for so long.

"Come Thou long expected Jesus, born to set Thy people free;
From our fears and sins release us; let us find our rest in Thee.
Israel's Strength and Consolation, hope
of all the earth, Thou art.
Dear desire of every nation, joy of every longing heart."[40]

What a strange way to save the world. God lives and acts "outside the box".

19

One Two Buckle my Shoe

Even having had all this truth bathe me in spa-like fashion, two nagging hangnails kept splintering my peace. Maybe you, too, have wondered....

Perplexing Puzzle One.

If Jesus really is all-powerful and all-knowing, why does He continue to allow immense suffering, pestilence, and injustice?

Arrogance abounds. The wicked prosper. Pride is worn as a necklace. Eyes bulge from fatness. Mockers tease. Tongues parade their fresh gossip. Garments of violence cover our cities. Godly values seem passé. Watching the six o'clock news we observe reactions to reports that a loved one had been murdered. "All I want is for justice to be served! Someone has to pay!" Yes, that's how God feels, too, but He dispatches payment on His schedule, not ours. And punishment is always *exactly* what is deserved.

But am I without sin myself? Is anyone? God's Eden *was* Paradise...before one sin. We earthlings cannot fathom or even begin to imagine what His perfection and Holiness truly are. Even one little slip-up...

Not anyone has never sinned; God doesn't keep a filing cabinet drawer categorizing "good" sins and "bad" sins. Pure. Chaste. Faultless. Blameless. Pristine. Consecrated. Utterly untainted. Hallowed. Divine. Cannot join country clubs or sororities; absolutely no biases or prejudices. Doesn't do touch-ups on our photographs; He doesn't need to: hypocrisy is not a game. Remakes anew, never caulks cracks. Holiness cannot see, hear, smell, taste, or touch anything with a spot of filth. We underestimate Who He is.

Like sap to a tree, so blood is to us. It is life. Blood was God's symbol for His justice. Someone must pay; sin must be obliterated. That's Who He is. Even though in the Old Testament animals' blood covered many an altar, it was only because of His mercy that He overlooked sin...for a season. The blood of a sheep or a ram or a dove was only a picture, a model, of what was truly needed: a perfect sacrifice.

Try to explain divorce to your child. See if he can understand the implications of leaving the freezer door wide open in August, after countless hours of garden labor. Interpret your 401K to a two year old. Let him drive your car. Define osmosis. Account for arguments among aunts and uncles who shun the family reunion. We are the young children here. No smidgen of our finite imagination can conceive of such an exalted, noble, lofty Being.

Another Wild Wrestling Match.
Why blood and a cross formed from two trees?
Couldn't God just whisper, "I'll clean it up" when we say, "uh-oh"?

In the fullness of God's beauty, wonder beyond wonders, He craves fellowship with each of us. If He took time to knit you in your mother's womb, you *know* that He loves you. "But, before we can understand the grace of God, we must first understand His wrath. Before we can understand His death, we *must* understand why His death was necessary. Before we can comprehend how loving, merciful, and gracious God is, we *must* first see how rebellious, sinful, and guilty mankind is."[41]

"Men do not act righteous because they are not rightly related to God. Because man's relationship to God is wrong, their relationship to their fellow man is wrong. Men treat other men the way they do because they treat God the way they do."[42]

So, because we choose to separate ourselves from Him, He devised a plan to redeem us, to buy us back, for the purpose of being able to commune with us. He *truly* delights in intimacy. He hungers to be "in-to-me". When someone purchases a birthday present, the gift is free to the recipient. It is not free to the giver because it costs to purchase that gift. And most of us take great care to select just the right gift, one that will not only please but delight the birthday girl or boy.

Because of His perfection, the only way of redeeming us would be a perfect sacrifice – a perfect gift. But because of sin and its curse on every person and on creation, there was no "thing" for Him to select. Sin leads to death; it demands that "someone pay".

Light is sown like seed for the righteous and gladness for the upright of heart." Psalm 97:11, NASB

So...for the unrighteous, anyone who does not "know" Christ intimately, darkness overtakes light. Anxiousness, frustration, anger, worry, agitation, fear.....all these befall us if we choose not to believe and obey.

Like Hansel and Gretel's bread crumbs thrown down to mark the path back home, life's pilgrimage will lead us to the wilderness, all our efforts being devoured by hungry birds. Their father abandoned his own children in the forest, but our Abba is forever ringing the dinner bell, "Supper's ready!"

"For the eyes of the Lord move to and fro throughout the whole earth, that He might strongly support those whose hearts are completely His." II Chronicles 16:9, NASB. When we choose Jesus, when we ask Him to buy us back, when "we confess with our mouth 'Jesus is Lord' (our salvation is secured) and believe in our heart that God raised Him from the dead (we are declared

righteous and can actually commune with Him), we are saved!"
Romans 10:9-10, NASB.

Watchman Nee in *The Normal Christian Life* says, "Our sins
were dealt with by the blood, we ourselves are dealt with by the
cross. The blood procures our pardon, the cross procures our
deliverance from what we are in Adam. The blood can wash away
my sins, but it cannot wash away my old man: I need the cross
to crucify me – the sinner."[43]

We are given a new nature; we are indeed brand-new
creatures, as II Corinthians 5:17 promises. God is the only One
who can DIY. He is not addicted to rehab. He is not a fixer-upper.
He doesn't love you or list you! No flip or flop. No rescuing "my"
renovation.

He starts from scratch- from the foundation. Our new nature
is, well, completely new. We smell like a new car to Him. Like
Susan, who passed by my high school study hall desk at 9:00
a.m. every morning, her cologne settled as a cloud that stationed
itself right over my desk. I never even looked up, for it didn't
matter what outfit she was arrayed in or how her hair had been
teased and combed. We are "Christ to God" (II Corinthians
2:15), the only Jesus someone might ever see. He is really truly
believably living *in me*!

We are not perfect...yet; that waits for heaven, but, if moment
by moment and day by day, we hook ourselves up to the Vine,
He orders our steps. Electricity must flow from the transformer.
A lamp must be plugged in to work. Phones must be charged to
operate. Babies are conceived when husbands and wives join
together as one. A seed must be buried in the dirt and watered;
it is only then that the hard outer shell cracks. One must be
immersed in His love letter – a living active tutor. The only
way for the Holy Spirit to exert His opus in us is for us to plug
ourselves in, into the Vine Jesus, "for apart from Me, you can do
nothing." John 15:5, NASB.

It's all hay, wood, and stubble – wasted effort. Kudzu choking our endeavors, labor pains that produce no baby, trials all resulting in guilty verdicts, vacuums sucking every piece of life that are not tied down. Every Monday is rainy. Dead fish lie rancid in the garbage. Purses and pockets develop holes in the bottom; rob Peter to pay Paul. Plug into power!

In our hurried frenzies, as we gerbils revolve around and around in our cages, as we instantly connect via social media, we lose. In trying to win the battle, we lose the war. Life was not made for us to fight DIY style, scratching and clawing through tasks, day by day, year into year, chore after chore, as we mark each undertaking off our calendar, all the while sinking deeper in the mire of our own garbage. Ouch!

Rest in His arms, muscular, but oh, so tender. I preach mostly to myself. Loosen the vise grips of control. Unwind the screw securing our preconceived plans. Slacken the ropes that choke weeds of discontent. Unmask hypocrisy and permit vulnerability that oozes its healing balm of unfettered joy. Recline in the fresh breeze of fatherly protection.

20

Something Old. Something New.

It's high time for a name change. Qaneh, the "Reed", like Abraham and Jacob, has morphed into a new creature. Just as Abba saw fit to rename His own to fit His purpose, I saw fit to rename this treasure that pulls me.

Not Abram: exalted father, but Abraham: father of multitudes.

Not Jacob: crafty, deceitful, and selfish; but Israel: faithful, obedient, prayerful, divinely disciplined.[44]

Not Simon, but Peter. Jesus proclaimed, "You are Peter (petros-stone), and upon this rock (petra-boulder) I will build My church." Matthew 16:18, NASB. Peter confessed his conviction in the Deity of Jesus. The "Rock" is the Truth that Jesus is the Son of God, and this is the foundation of the church.[45]

Not Qaneh: the reed that shakes in the wind; but Marturia: a testimony, one bearing witness.[46]

Marturia, like myself, is exhibiting age spots. Spider veins branch out like the manner of markings on a broken windshield, first a pebble point, next a plethora of directional fingers, marring youthful pinkness. Proverbs says that gray hair is a crown of glory (16:31), but we still spend megabucks to conceal its lesson to younger moms.

Certainly television commercials and magazine ads promote youth and rake in untold millions with promises of fewer wrinkles, more energy, and alluring multi-colored counterfeit nails. Marturia's hearth has grown cold; fireflies give off light with no one delighting to catch the glow; the well that once quenched thirst has long been abandoned; sleet, rain, and frigid air dance between fractured window panes. But the little boy/man cannot tear her down just yet. She is a witness, a testimony to him of a grand rescue. His grandparents paid a ransom to redeem that orphan, sacrificing the empty nest to love the homeless.

Autumn's gifts are a cornucopia of beauty and coziness, but it is a period of maturation (like me and Marturia) and the beginning of decline. However, albeit knowing that winter is nipping at its heels, autumn produces a glory that cannot be detected in March. The world seems to slow down to watch as the sap voids life in the leaves. Is there is anything in God's creation like the explosive delight and charm of golds, reds, oranges, and yellows as they rest on their deathbed?

But God deals in paradox. Life springs from death. Success is delivered only through failure. Even so, the seasons march us from infancy to middle age to elderliness, each one parading their precious pristine treasures but also their tainted unwholesome treasons; both offer abundant prizes if we are hungry to search long and hard. The fall seeds that have been cast to the ground are cozy in the fallen leaves and dirt, but the cost is great, for in order to spring to life once again, the seed corn must die. El Shaddai must nurture and coax it to grow.

From the day its hardness is broken in secret, until the giant tree's roots decay, and it topples over to be food for new growth, many many dawns and sunsets have lapsed. Seasons come; seasons go. Through oppressive heat and bitter cold, through drought and monsoons, through sap rising and leaves modeling His glory, the tree has stood tall, giving fruit and shade to the weary.

Weeds surrounding the tree have no such struggle. Look at untended Marturia; thorns and thistles have usurped useful garden plots, and vine tentacles continue to suck the life out of her.

But that's not who she is in her core. She still stands as a testimony, a witness of what she was: a HOME. Children playing games. Grandma hanging clothes on the line. Daddy comin' in after a hard day to greet Mama with a kiss. Winter nights by the fire. Summer nights on the porch shellin' peas. Saturday night rituals. Company after church on Sunday. A sanctuary of kissed boo-boos and teenage love gone awry.

As Marturia ages, so do we. But this death trap we look at each morning in the mirror is not who we are either. If we do not *know* (personally, deeply) Jesus, we still live in our old selfish fleshly tent. We sprang from Adam, and, like Adam, we fell into spiritual death (Romans 5:19)... like it or not. Realizing that we *do* sin, are totally self-centered, and consistently do what we don't want to do and don't do what we know we should do, is *not* making us stronger but weaker. A peculiar way to victory?

Christ's resurrection is also our resurrection to a new life, a new nature. Because we still live inside this death trap, we will still sin, but, by plugging in and daily entreating for His life to live in and through us, we are freed to be holy. Our enemy within is our old nature, fighting for control. But, we have clothed ourselves with His robe, and the new creation is the victor every time we yield. Inside, in the heart, a hive of sorts, is where He lives. We choose die to our hard selves, so our old desires crack and crumble; then by His gift of Bread and Living Water, new seedlings sprout up, reaching for Sonshine!

It is through His paradoxical plan that our roots, planted downward by struggles and need, cause us to grow upward in intimacy and praise. God's scheme is that victory comes through weaknesses, failures, and defeats. He craves voluntary crucifixion to our circumstances, so that we discover our destiny only by divine sustenance. He crucifies the old man, not by helping him, but by removing him from the scene of action to a spectacular new view. The beauty of autumn is in the dying, secure in the knowledge that one day, in the not-too-distant future, spring's re-creation will surely arrive.

Testament. Witness. Evidence. Attestation. Proof. Confirmation. Declaration. Old Testament. New Testament.

My appropriating, my reaching out to receive the reality of this faith, has taken years, Y – E – A – R - S. In my own guilt over major poor choices some thirty years ago and in the actuality of how my older two boys' lives were forever altered, Abba handed me a grand opportunity on my faith journey – DIY or "Let Me." Because they were "my" failures, I intimated that I had to be their Savior. There are no "conditions" or "commandments" that I must follow to gain His favor. I am not their Holy Spirit. Yes, I was a new creation living in a DIY mind-set. "But God, who is rich in mercy, because of His great love with which He loved us, even when we were dead in our trespasses, made us alive together with Christ (by grace you have been saved)." Ephesians 2: 4, NKJ. Mercy doesn't give us the whippin' we deserve, and grace frees us to respond to His wooing, whatever He bids us do.

Get that? **You** are His opus. And He will not stop loving and goading **His own** children until His purpose for creating us is finished. His own adopted ones are those children who have tugged on the hem of His robe, gazed into His tender eyes, raised their hands to be picked up, and have delightfully accepted His invitation to be our Abba through Jesus' bloody perfect sacrifice. In Eden there were no orphans. Yes, everything the Father has is ours. Yes, our inheritance is plentiful. Yes, eternal life is sure, but Abba will only deposit Himself fully in those who are truly passionate and unctuous about taking firm hold of His life.

Remember my fervent plea to **'Hold that Thought'** in chapter 18, just after God had changed Abram's name to exhibit that He meant business about setting up the Jews as His witness? Time to let her rip!

We cannot physically see the life in an apple seed, even though God has already determined its objective, appearance, and fruit. So, too, He has already woven us together in the depths of the earth and knows His intention for us deep inside this death trap of a tent.

All through His living Word we see His great compassion for drawing His children close to His breast. Over and over: rebellion, judgment, redemption. The washing machine repeats its task: agitating; draining, then spinning all the filth away; bearing clean clothes, all spots removed.

In one especially poignant Old Testament book, Hosea ("deliverance")[47] the prophet (the herald of a divine message)[48], marries a prostitute. God speaks of His spiritual marriage to Israel through the physical marriage of Gomer and Hosea, so that we can plainly relate to His sorrow when we shun His advances and His desire to take us to Himself. In a courtroom scene, charges are brought against the defendant: "She doesn't know it was I who gave her new grain...and lavished on her silver and gold." Hosea 2:8, NASB. Gomer took Hosea for granted, just like Israel was presuming on her Father.

"I will uncover her lewdness in the sight of her lovers, and no one will rescue her out of my hand. I will put an end to her gaiety... and destroy the vines that give her wages." Hosea 2:10-12, NASB. God's desire (as Hosea's heart) was to have her see her need of Him. The Father offers to bring the entire dowry: "Then I will allure (woo) her in the wilderness and speak kindly to her. I will betroth her to me in righteousness and justice." 2:14, 19, NASB.

The land mourned, the people languished over troubled times. Priests led people astray. Rulers were reeking with rottenness. God grievously stated that He would remove His hand of protection "until they acknowledge their guilt and seek My face; in their affliction they will earnestly seek Me." 5:15, NASB.

The Jews repented and vowed to "press on to know the Lord." 6:3, NASB.

No sooner had His healing touch been received than the nation once again went about their worldly business. No one realized that God was judging them, so again they "sowed to the wind". 8:7. Hosea foretold the lack of joy, the exile into Babylon, which did indeed happen before his death.

"Sow for yourselves righteousness, reap in mercy; break up your fallow ground, for it is time to seek the Lord, till He comes and rains righteousness on you." 10:12, NKJ.

Chapter 11 tears at a mother's heartstrings as Hosea laments over his lost lover. "When Israel was a child, I loved him." (v 1) But His love wouldn't put them on a leash. "I taught Israel to walk, taking them in My arms, but they never knew that I healed them. I led them... with ropes of kindness... I bent down to give them food." (v 3-4) Even though He rocked them and sang over them, they rebelled, over and over. Mercy, however, has its limits. The wound up clock runs out of spunk. So God found it necessary to take harsh steps to rein His children in. War began to swirl through their cities; their enemies began to trap them in their own evil plans. And the people wondered how a good God could allow such troubles. "We go to church, we throw our coins in the offering plate, we raise our hands and recite the Scripture." All the while God cries, "Yes, they call on Me, but no one exalts Me. How can I give you up? How can I hand you over?... My heart churns within Me, and My sympathy is stirred. No, I will not execute the fierceness of My anger...for I am God, and not man, the Holy One in your midst." 11: 7-9, NKJ.

Hosea relays that the Jews were crafty merchants selling from dishonest scales (12:7), and their paychecks were frivolously spent on carnal pleasures (v 8). However, they licked the sweet icing off this "fashionable iniquity", rationalizing that "It's just what one does to get ahead." Reputations were left intact...for a season. *Does this sound familiar?* Like *today's* world? EXACTLY! Remember. Repent. Return in righteousness. Could we allow ourselves the time and vulnerability of mourning with Him? Could we even begin to know His pain? Or will we continue to dance with the world, pull warm blankets of comfort around our sated bellies, and stop up our ears with media, baseball/dance practices, and sporting stats so that we cannot hear the Goliath of hurts and loneliness?

Because of His covenant promises to Abraham and David, He *will* return to bless Israel. The scattered seeds which have been blown to the earth's four corners by the winter winds will find themselves once again blooming in their native soil. I AM *is* the providing Shelter: the cross covers us. "Whoever is wise, let him understand these things....for the ways of the Lord are right, and the righteous will walk in them. But transgressors will stumble in them.." (v 14:9), NASB.

His holiness requires justice; He is too chaste to don a saddle over our tolerance. *But...*because of His great mercy He loiters; it is His kindness that is patient, waiting for hearts to turn to Him.

But...one day His wrath *will* even the score! For years, seemingly for eons, people lived in darkness, waiting, w–a–i–t–i–n-g, on the Light, wondering when God would send their Deliverer. Then, in the fullness of His time, Jesus did come, extremely slow as we mortals would consider time and in the dirtiest dustiest lowliest place. Not even a stop sign in Bethlehem.

I write this only after He has consistently and continually pressed me in His vise. "Who cares? Stories abound these days."

"Everyone seems to be tooting horns, heralding accounts of their favorite anecdotes."

"Narratives and opinions and forwarded fancies flood Facebook. Why pick up a book, when drama's floodgates appear on reality PCs?

"Among all the twittering and blogging and instagrams this yarn doesn't have a chance!" Sorry about that thought, Lord.

"Jill, lest you forget: 'Nothing is too difficult for Me, nothing is too difficult for Me; ah, I the Lord God have made the heavens and the earth by My great power and My outstretched arms.' Jeremiah 32:17, NASB, paraphrased. 'Not by might, nor by power, but by My Spirit.' Zechariah 4:6. 'You did not choose Me, but I chose you, and appointed you, that you should go and bear fruit'.... John 15:16, NASB."

Because, like His chosen ones in Deuteronomy 7:8, He "brought me out with a mighty hand and redeemed me from slavery", from my wanderings and strongholds of opinions and viewpoints, I cannot NOT proclaim Him. It is not to say that I have by any means arrived at the depot, but I am beginning to grasp His hand more tightly. On the days that I lounge in His shadow, I feel His favor.

An unsettling dream kept recurring for months. I was teaching again but not with all my heart in it, not preparing lessons well, just going through the motions. Panic waves would rivet me awake. Given responsibility for 25 or so children's lives for nine months worried me into a stew, but I couldn't seem to keep from procrastination, from just taking baby steps to "just do it". Months passed while I filed my nails and played "Drop the Handkerchief", which guided these children down a dead-end path to nowhere. The nightmare was in my closet, but I was too frozen to banish him.

Classroom settings changed night after night, the people as varied as polka-dots, but the principal finally called me in. Caught with my hand in the cookie jar! Cautiously cracking open her office door, my eyes witnessed a benevolent "yes" face behind this capacious desk, which was catty-cornered on the opposite wall. Floor to ceiling glass windowpanes converged behind her chair. It was as if she sat in a TV studio with masses of Times Square humanity scurrying all around, each human resolved to reach his personal destination. Everyone was oblivious to the din, for individual agendas danced in each psyche.

What a perch from which to people watch! But she only had eyes for me. Moving timidly forward, my focus was stealthily welded on how extremely filthy dirty the window was. Why would a CEO in an executive office allow dark clouds to mar her view of the sunshine?

I sat before my supervisor, caught red-handed, my feet sinking in miry clay. I was unprepared, not ready. Qualified, yet unfit. Furnished with a mission, yet unwilling to fulfill my task. No excuse. Nada. Night after night. I dreaded sleep but was unyielding in seeking relief from the One who transported me to Where the Wild Things Are.

The way up is down. The way to victory is through a battle. The way to healing is brokenness. 5:00 a.m. – very *very* early for a night-owl. Enough is enough. Depositing myself on the bottom bunk in an abandoned bedroom, I propped myself up to wrestle with God.

Me and God had a heart-to-heart chat. "If You don't relieve me, I am toast! I give up. Surrender. Wave the white flag. Call uncle as I wait for the Pawnbroker to exchange my grief and anxiety for His prescribed meds. No audible voice ever came, but He spoke volumes.

"You are not ready for Me. Your field lies fallow. The dirty window is sin in your life, keeping Me at arm's length. You are always so organized but never unmasked with Me or with others. DIY gals never permit interruptions of your "to-do" lists. See the outline of many hurried people on the outside; however, you can't see them clearly because you've been unwilling to come clean with Me. Why, just gaze at all the worry and guilt you shoulder! Don't you know I can –and want – to shoulder that burden for you? Come HOME. 'Come to Me, all you who are weary and heavy laden, and *I will* give you rest. Take *My* yoke upon you; learn from *Me*. **I am** gentle and humble in heart, and you *shall* find rest for your souls'." Matthew 11:28-29, NASB, emphasis mine.

Hmm...tranquility from *all* my daily...mundane...common... repetitive activities. Abba had already told Jeremiah (6:16, HCSB) many years before to tell the Jews to "stand by the roadways and look. Ask about the ancient paths: Which is the way to what is good? Then take it and find rest for yourselves."

"He who has found his life shall lose it, and he who has lost his life for *My* sake shall find it." Matthew 10:39, NASB.

"You're so busy being perfect that you're driving those who need Me away. How can they see *Me* in *you* if all they see is you? And, not only are you sinning, but the masses moving to and fro on the outside need Me, too! If you play in the mud, you get dirty, but you also sling it on your surroundings. How will they know Me if no one tells them?

I AM your Principal. I do not condemn you, but go HOME. Prepare your heart. Then come. I stand at the window, curtains pulled back, intently gazing down the path for My prodigal to come for supper. The hearth is warm. My rocking chair is beckoning. The light in the window glows steadily and surely.

I remember your unctuous prayer over 25 years ago...'Please give me a testimony'."

I AM is Your witness. This is His-story.

Only four tenths of a mile away Marturia remains propped up. So close. I've been there all along, watching you grow older on the outside, but that's not who you are. **I AM** living on the inside, waiting daily for you to come HOME.

Resurrection is only an autumn away. I already know what is inside that seed corn: a fair and lovely rose. Relax. Let it fall... right into My arms, for *you* are my first-hand witness.

"And the Spirit and the bride (church) say, 'Come.' And let those who hear say, 'Come.' And let the thirsty come; let the one who wishes take the water of life without cost." (Rev. 22:17, NASB)

Write. Share. Love.

ENDNOTES

1. Joan Gale Thomas, *If Jesus Came to my House* (New York: Lothrop, Lee, and Shepherd, Co., Inc., 1951).
2. W. E. Vine, *Vine's Complete Expository Dictionary of Old and New Testament Words* (Nashville: Thomas Nelson, Inc., 1996), 516.
3. Ron Dunn, sermon "God's Surprises", Travis Avenue Baptist Church, Fort Worth, TX, April 11, 1995.
4. Dr. David Jeremiah, as heard on radio FM 106, Asheville, NC, 1990.
5. William M. McElrath, *A Bible Dictionary for Young Readers* (Nashville: Broadman Press,1965),86.
6. Ron Dunn, sermon "Three Crises of Faith", First Baptist Church, Hattiesburg, MS, 2000.
7. Margery Williams, *The Velveteen Rabbit* (New York: Camelot Books, 1975), 17.
8. Randy Pausch, *The Last Lecture* (Hyperion Books, 2008), 25.
9. Matthew Henry, *Matthew Henry's Commentary on the Whole Bible, Vol. 3* (Peabody, MA: Hendrickson Publishing, 1992), 436.
10. Oswald Chambers, *My Utmost for His Highest*, ed. James Reiman (Nashville: Thomas Nelson Co., 1992), October 11.
11. Sarah Hart and Chapin Hartford, "Better Than a Hallelujah", sung by Amy Grant
12. Ron Dunn, sermon "Faith's Tests", Travis Avenue Baptist Church, Fort Worth, TX, April, 1995.
13. Ibid.
14. Merrill F. Unger, *Unger's Concise Bible Dictionary* (Grand Rapids: Baker Book House, 1989), 171.
15. Gertrude Crampton, *Tootle the Train* (Racine, WI: Western Publishing Co., 1945).

16. Clement C. Moore, *The Night Before Christmas* (Racine, WI: Western Publishing Co., Eleventh Printing, 1973)
17. Oswald Chambers, *My Utmost for His Highest*, ed. James G. Reimann (Grand Rapids, MI, Discovery House Publishers, 1992), April 29 devotional.
18. Phillip Dodridge, song lyrics, "O, Happy Day", 1775
19. Jerry Bridges, *Trusting God* (Colorado Springs, CO: NavPress, 1988), 192.
20. Randy Pausch, *The Last Lecture* (Hyperion Books, 2008).
21. John MacArthur, *MacArthur Bible Commentary* (Nashville: Thomas Nelson, Co., 2005), 838.
22. Miles Stanford, *The Green Letters* (Zondervan, 1983), 36.
23. John MacArthur, *The MacArthur New Testament Commentary, Romans 1-8* (Chicago, Moody Press, 1991), 462.
24. Dan Allender, *The Wounded Heart: Hope for Adult Victims of Childhood Sexual Abuse* (Colorado Springs, CO: NavPress, 1990), 180.
25. Dee Brestin, *Friendships of Women* (Wheaton, IL: Victor Books, 1995), 157.
26. Paraphrased from "Shackles", sung by Mary, Mary; Thankful Mary Mary CD, April Music, Inc., 2000.
27. Erwin McManus, *Soul Cravings* (Nashville: Thomas Nelson, 2006), Entry 15: "Where Do I Belong?"
28. Carolyn Walz Kramlich, *Mary's Treasure Box* (Nashville, Thomas Nelson, Inc., 1998).
29. W. E. Vines, *Vine's Complete Expository Dictionary of Old and New Testament Words* (Nashville: Thomas Nelson, Inc., 1996), 476.
30. Ibid., 385.
31. William Law, quoted in *The Green Letters,* Miles Stanford (Zondervan, 1983), 36.
32. Joseph Stowell, *Following Christ* (Zondervan, 1998), 80.
33. Dee Brestin, *Friendships of Women* (Wheaton, IL: Victor Books, 1995), 21.
34. Merrill Unger, *Unger's Concise Bible Dictionary* (Grand Rapids: Baker House, 1989), 115.
35. Lucinda McDowell, *Quilts from Heaven* (Nashville: Broadman and Holman, 1999), quoted "From Where Love Resides", 53. Used by permission.
36. Ingrid Trobish, "Keeper of the Springs", quoted in *Quilts From Heaven* (Broadman Holman, 1996), 55. Used by permission.

37. Eugene Fields, "The Sugar-Plum Tree", from scraps of a book that my mama cherished when she was young, read to us girls every Christmas Eve, too loved to provide any information.

38. Margery Williams, *The Velveteen Rabbit* (New York, Doubleday Books, 1975),15.

39. Kay Arthur, *Finding Covenant: God's Enduring Promises* (Nashville, Lifeway Publishing, 2009), 212.

40. Charles Wesley, song lyrics to "Come Thou Long Expected Jesus", 1744

41. John MacArthur, *Commentary on the New Testament Romans 1-9* (Chicago, Moody Press, 1991),75.

42. Ibid, 67.

43. Watchman Nee, *The Normal Christian Life* (Tyndale House, 1977), 25.

44. W. E. Vine, *Vine's Complete Expository Dictionary* (Nashville: Thomas Nelson, 1996), 9, 98.

45. Henry Halley, *Halley's Bible Handbook* (Zondervan, Twenty-fourth ed., 1965), 441.

46. W. E. Vine, *Vine's Complete Expository Dictionary* (Nashville: Thomas Nelson, 1996),681.

47. Merrill F. Unger, *Unger's Concise Bible Dictionary* (Grand Rapids, MI: Baker House, 1989), 93.

48. W. E. Vine, *Vine's Complete Expository Dictionary* (Nashville: Thomas Nelson, 1996), 493.

Bibles Used

1. *New American Standard Bible* (NASB) (Nashville: Holman Bible Publishers, 1985).

2. *Holman Christian Standard Bible* (HCSB) (Nashville: Holman Bible Publishers, 2008).

3. *The Believer's Study Bible, New King James Version* (NKJ) (Nashville: Thomas Nelson Publishers, 1991).

Printed in the United States
By Bookmasters